W9-DGS-811

A Rainbow Book

Praise for *Watch It!*

"*Watch It!* reminds thoughtful parents of the dangers media can present to their children. Unlike other books on the subject, *Watch It!* adds practical suggestions for the busy parent on how to protect their children from the adverse effects of over-exposure to the media.

"It is the intelligent parents' guide to the ill effects of the mass media. As an educator who teaches media literacy in the classroom, this book reminds me of how we are on the same page. It is our children who benefit — and they need to."

—Martha Cosgrove, Minnesota Council of Teachers of English Teacher of the Year, 2006

"Mary Larson delivers on the title's promise—*What Parents Need to Know*. Her book is easy to read, based on solid research, and filled with practical suggestions you can use today. This is a great resource for the 21st century parent."

—David Walsh, Ph.D., founder of the National Institute on Media and the Family and author of *No. Why Kids of All Ages Need to Hear It and Ways Parents Can Say It*

"Your book is engaging, comprehensive and an eye-opener to parents and educators alike. We have included Media Literacy in our curriculum; research indicates it is an important part of our students' lives, and schools have an important role in helping students develop critical skills about the Media. However, your book made me realize how much broader than simply TV and the internet the Media is for our students.

continued

"Your book also clearly underscores how important it is for our teachers to have a close partnership with parents and our community.

"Frankly, I plan on giving a copy of your book as a baby gift to every new parent I know! And the "What You Can Do" suggestions are doable and practical and any caring parent with children of all ages can benefit from trying them."

—Eileen Johnson, Curriculum Specialist for Language Arts and Social Studies, Edina MN Public Schools

Watch It!

What Parents Need to Know to Raise Media-Smart Kids

MARY STROM LARSON, ED.D.

Rainbow Books, Inc.
FLORIDA

Library of Congress Cataloging-in-Publication Data

Larson, Mary Strom.
  Watch it! : what parents need to know to raise media-smart kids /
Mary Strom Larson.
    p. cm.
  Includes bibliographical references.
  ISBN 1-56825-109-2 (trade softcover : alk. paper)
  1. Television and children—United States. 2. Television and family—
United States. 3. Mass media and children—United States. 4.
Parenting—United States. 5. Parent and child—United States. I. Title.
  HQ784.T4L38 2008
  302.23'450830973—dc22
                              2007045134

Watch It!
What Parents Need to Know to Raise Media-Smart Kids

Copyright 2009 © Mary Strom Larson

ISBN-10: 1-56825-109-2
ISBN-13: 978-1-56825-109-7

Published by Rainbow Books, Inc.

Editorial Offices

P. O. Box 430 • Highland City, FL 33846-0430
Telephone (863) 648-4420 • Fax: (863) 647-5951
RBIbooks@aol.com • www.RainbowBooksInc.com

Individuals' Orders

Toll-free orders: 1-800-431-1579
www.Amazon.com • www.AllBookStores.com

The paper used in this publication meets the minimum requirements of
the American National Standard for Information Sciences—Permanence
of Paper for Printed Library Materials, ANSI Z39.48-1984.

13 12 11 10 09   5 4 3 2 1

First Edition, 2009
Printed in the United States of America.

To Ingrid and Martha,
who got me started on this venture,
and Charlie,
who helped me get it to fruition.

Contents

* Billboard sign in South Dakota

Preface

I began my serious study of TV some years ago when my two daughters were in junior high. As parents of junior high school girls know, they can be the meanest, most unpleasant creatures alive. My daughters communicated with each other using snarls, catty comments and compliments that were insults in disguise ("What a cool sweater," was said dripping with sarcasm). In a fit of pique, I muttered, "It must be that darned TV set!" Then it hit me: Maybe it really was the television set. As an educator, I have been researching and teaching about how the media shapes the minds of our children and families ever since.

In the years I have taught about the effects of the media, many of my students have also been parents. At the end of the semester they would often comment that the course had profoundly changed the way they look at the media. They told me that I needed to reach a larger audience than fifteen or twenty students a semester, and, at their urging, I finally sat down and wrote this book.

.

Introduction

A recent *Frontline* documentary profiled nine-year-old Paul, who lives in a rough part of a large city.[1] On summer mornings he tunes in *Power Rangers* on his bedroom TV as soon as he wakes up. After a nine-minute break for breakfast, he washes up and heads back to his TV for cartoons, game shows and *Gilligan's Island*. He watches until his mom calls him for a quick lunch, which is followed by more TV. The soaps bore him, and he doesn't have cable, so he channel surfs or plays in the back yard with his younger brother until they're over. After dinner, he plops down for *Batman, Married with Children*, and *COPS*. Paul's Mom encourages the constant watching; she's scared that if he's out in the neighborhood, bigger boys will beat him up or talk him into trouble. She especially wants him to watch *COPS*; she thinks it teaches him what will happen if he breaks the law.

Although Paul's time with TV is unusual, the average American child watches TV for about three hours a day[2] and spends more than five hours a day with other types of media—computers, radios, and video games.[3] Close to ninety-nine percent of Americans own at least one TV set,[4] and those who choose not to own a TV are exposed to it in doctors' waiting rooms, airports, sports bars, restaurants, and the appliance departments at places like Wal-Mart. Even parents who work hard to control what their kids watch often fail at it. In addition, more than two-thirds of children over age eight have TV sets in their own bedrooms.[5] What these kids watch in private would likely shock their parents. Children's typical choices include sleazy afternoon talk shows, featuring such things as mothers who are having sex with their daughters' boyfriends. Prime time programs, such as *Friends*, and cable TV's offerings, such as the *Howard Stern* show, are clearly targeted to adults but are surely watched by kids.

Long before Americans worried about TV's influence on kids, they worried about the effects of other mass media such as movies and comic books. Serious study of television began following the assassinations of President Kennedy, Malcolm X, Martin Luther King, Jr., and Robert Kennedy in the 1960s, when Lyndon Johnson formed a Presidential commission to determine the causes and prevention of violence. In 1969, an advisory committee was created to study the effects of television violence on the attitudes and behavior of kids and teens.[6] Since then, more than 3,000 studies have found a connection between watching TV violence and acting violently.[7]

In a joint statement in September of 2002, the American Medical Association, the American Psychological Association, the American Academy of Pediatrics and the American Academy of Child and Adolescent Psychiatry announced to Congress that "watching violent entertainment can lead to 'increases in aggressive attitudes, values and behavior, particularly in children."[8] In one of the most dreadful examples, a twelve-year-old boy killed his playmate in 1999 by imitating what he'd seen on pro wrestling.[9]

Contrary to what one might imagine, kids often don't get aggressive immediately after watching violent TV. Instead they store what they see as "scripts" for future use. When kids encounter unfamiliar situations, ones that seem like something they saw on TV, they may "call up" these scripts and use them in real life.

Although violence on television has gotten a lot of press, TV teaches kids about much more. It also shows them how to behave in families, courtship, sexual relationships, conversations, and gender roles. In short, TV shows kids how to act in the real world.

In addition to teaching kids about expected behavior, TV also tells them what to expect in the real world. For example, a detective who was a consultant to the writers of *NYPD Blue* explained in a radio interview that TV shows have shaped people's expectations about what happens in interrogation rooms. Therefore, in a real interrogation, a "TV" statement like "Now we'll get down to business" will effectively terrify a suspect.[10] In the case of TV violence, people who watch of a lot of TV may believe that the world is scarier than it really is, and they tend to adjust their own behavior accordingly.

TV also tells viewers what to expect about how men will treat women, what college will be like, how sexually active "normal" is, and how people of various racial and ethnic backgrounds differ from each other with outright or subliminal words or methods.

Not only does TV portray a distorted picture of real life, it also influences how people attach importance to events, issues and possessions. The most frequently aired news stories are often not the most important, but people think they are. Studies of media coverage of the Presidential political campaign of 1968 and continuing to the present, have found that the news shaped voters' perceptions of what were the most important issues in the campaign.[11]

The media also influence viewers' opinions of health issues. For example, after Katie Couric's husband died of colon cancer in 1998, Couric began promoting colon cancer prevention on the *Today Show*. Researchers credit her campaign with increasing the number of colonoscopies by 19 percent. Indeed, doctors call this increase the "Couric Effect."[12] Another powerful example of media's effect on viewer behavior is Oprah's Book Club. Before Oprah Winfrey discontinued the club in 2002, books that she featured sold at least 500,000 more copies than the publishers had originally predicted.[13]

Kids are marketed as much as or more than adults are. Commercials convince kids that if they don't have the right designer jeans or the right video game, they won't have friends. Kids say they feel they have to have certain products and that having the "right stuff" makes them feel good about themselves.[14] Many kids do not understand that commercials are paid TV time and not part of the program they're watching. They don't realize that the kids in commercials are actors who might not like or use the toy or video game that's being advertised.

What You Can Do

This book does not advocate that people get rid of their TV sets. That's just not going to happen. But this book does highlight the likely consequences of kids consuming television without adult intervention. It's easy for adults to say, "My kid knows the difference between the TV world and the real world," and think their kids are protected from the influence of the tube. Knowing the differences is not the same as being immune to TV's effects. This book presents strategies for mitigating some of TV's problematic impacts on children.

Chapter 1

Whatever Happened to *Ozzie and Harriet?*

Life in Television Families

In the early days of television, Harriet Nelson of *Ozzie and Harriet* cleaned the house in a dress and high heeled shoes like most other TV mothers of those days. The glamorous Harriet even wore a mink coat when she went shopping. Although I was a reasonably bright ten-year-old, I firmly believed that my mother, who cleaned the house in jeans and tennis shoes and had no mink coat, was a drip. The mothers of my friends also wore jeans and tennis shoes, which should have tipped me off that Harriet was unrealistic, but I simply assumed that our whole neighborhood was full of drips. Even in those days, television affected children's ideas about how real-life families should be.

My story illustrates the fact that the media tell kids what to expect from real life. You may be thinking: "My kid knows the difference between TV and real life." However, up until about the age of eight, kids really are not able to distinguish between fantasy and reality. So they actually don't know the difference between TV and real life. Also, it is a commonly held misperception that "other kids may be influenced by TV, but my kid isn't." Interestingly, virtually all parents have this belief.

When parents are asked: "How much does TV influence your child?" they respond: "Not very much." When asked: "How much does TV influence other kids?" they respond: "Quite a lot." How can it be that TV doesn't influence everybody's kids at the same time it does influence everybody else's kids? The fact is that everybody's kids are influenced, including yours.

Today, kids watching television still believe their moms and dads should act like the ones they see on their favorite programs. Kids in single parent families watch intact families on TV to see what it's like to be in a two-parent family. Children without siblings look to TV to tell them what it would be like to have a sister or brother. So we must look critically at what family life is like in television families. We must look past the pratfalls and ignore the laugh track and objectively analyze what television moms, dads and kids do and don't do in their families.

TV also gives kids ideas about how they should behave in their own families, and kids often imitate what they see on TV. Kids who smart off to their parents may well have learned this behavior from a kid on TV. Children learn from TV how to be a sibling, and even a parent when the time comes. In 1989, popular psychologist Dr. Joyce Brothers recommended that parents imitate Claire and Cliff Huxtable of *The Cosby Show* if they wanted to be better parents.[1] Was this really such a good idea? Were the Huxtables the ideal parents?

In Defense of *The Simpsons*

Is it possible that Marge and Homer Simpson are better models for parenting than Claire and Cliff Huxtable? Early criticisms of the program suggested that Homer and Marge were horrible parents. When *The Simpsons* first came on the air, they were called dysfunctional and referred to as a "grungy, bickering lot," typical of the "squalid underbelly of life."[2] Interestingly, my own academic research contradicts that description. In fact, statistical analyses of family interactions on the show found that Homer and Marge are better parents than Cliff and Claire in many ways.[3]

Most importantly, the Simpson family is one in which the parents are in charge. Marge doesn't ask whether or not the kids want to go to church. She tells them: "Get your butts down here! We're going to church!" In the early 1960s women's magazines advocated the idea of a "family council." This was the idea that the family would get together and make decisions together. But at present the notion has gotten out of hand. Some decisions are better made without child input— what model car to buy, how expensive a family vacation can we plan, which house to buy. Parents are the family members with the life experiences that qualify them to make many family decisions unilaterally.

As one might expect from a cohesive family, *The Simpsons* are involved in community life. In one episode, Homer worried about a dangerous street corner in town. Upset, he decided to take action. He planned his case, took it to the City Council, and got a traffic light installed on the corner. In another episode, Marge became outraged with the amount of violence she saw on kids' television. She actually conducted a content analysis of violent acts on *Krusty the Clown* and took her complaints to the sponsors, demanding they put pressure on the networks to stop the violence.

Indeed, both Homer and Marge take active roles in the lives of their children. Homer helped Lisa reckon with the disappointment of not getting the starring role in the school play and explained that all parts, big and small, are important. In another program, Homer, wanting Bart to fit in at the "gifted school," taught him how to wear a tie. When Lisa was sad because she wasn't accepted by the popular kids, Marge reassured her that she should be her own person, no matter what. *The Simpsons* also do things together, such as sit down for meals, play Scrabble and go to the company picnics at the nuclear power plant. Clearly, the Simpson family offers many positive roles for family life.

Rather than forbid kids to watch *The Simpsons*, parents and children should watch the program together and talk about the family interactions. My daughters and I enjoyed watching this show together. We talked about how Bart defended Lisa against the bullies at school, and we decided that this was a valuable thing for a brother to do for his sister. TV offered the lesson, but as a parent I could direct the learning.

An Attack on *The Brady Bunch*

TV sitcoms go through cycles, and in the 1960s "blended" families featured prominently in the line up. *The Brady Bunch*, for example, was an enormously popular show. In fact, my college students can reenact entire episodes verbatim. The show, still available in syndication, featured a newly married widow and widower, and their combined children. While the kids engaged in minor skirmishes, for the most part the Brady clan was a stress-free family. Unlike real stepfamilies, the blended families on TV in the '60s and '70s were usually made up of parents who had been widowed, conveniently avoiding issues like visitation rights or custody battles. In these TV families, no kid said things like, "You're not my mom—you can't tell me what to do!"

In reality, parents in blended families find that there is a long, stressful period during which new relationships are forged, and sometimes these relationships are not forged at all. For instance, the sibling who was formerly the oldest and got certain privileges may now be the third oldest, losing "rank." Children often feel jealous of the attention paid to the new spouse and believe that they are no longer as important.

Overall, kids who get their ideas about blended families from television are getting an unrealistic view of what these families are like in real life. Children in real stepfamilies may believe that their family is weird or that they have done something wrong because their family relationships are difficult. Again, parents who assume that their children's expectations about blended families are not influenced by what they see on TV are mistaken.

From Claire to Marge; from Cliff to Homer: Family Roles on Television

A closer look at additional television families tells us how family roles are played out on television. Viewers are provided models of mothering, fathering and siblingship. They also develop expectations of how their family members should behave and perform.

Mothers

Harriet Nelson made me think my 1950's mother was a drip for cleaning in jeans and sneakers. In the 1980s and later, many television mothers had successful, high-visibility careers and spent little if any time cleaning the house. Let's take a critical look at more current TV moms and what they do and don't do. Mothers like Elyse Keaton, the architect on *Family Ties*, juggled career and motherhood without much trouble. Indeed, viewers rarely, if ever, saw those TV moms frazzled at the tough jobs of being career woman and mother. We rarely saw her actually doing architectural work, so the toll that jobs take on working moms was not there. In the real world, work and family constantly clash for women. We also rarely saw her doing the scut work of mothering—cleaning toilets, sweeping floors, cleaning cupboards.

Obviously, these activities would not make for very attractive television. But children of real life working moms may see their moms as less than adequate for being stressed by the career-family juggling act. And, again, we cannot assume that any normal kid would intuitively know that TV and real life are not alike.

In addition to creating unrealistic expectations about mothers, successful working moms on television offer another problem. Young women, modeling their aspirations after these TV characters, often end up disillusioned by their inability to pull off the two roles. Denise, an attorney in her early 30s, once hoped to make partner at a high-powered law firm. To accomplish this goal, she worked 60-hour weeks and took much work home on weekends. She was ecstatic when her baby boy was born; but when her maternity leave ended, she saw it would be impossible to be both the mother and the attorney she wanted to be. With great difficulty, she returned to her earlier teaching career that, although time consuming and difficult, allowed her to do some of her work at home. Though she believes she made the right choice, she still feels inadequate that she couldn't do it all.

The pervasiveness of the "supermom" on television probably had something to do with Denise's expectations about combining career and motherhood. She told me that it angered her that Claire Huxtable made juggling a career as an attorney and mother to five children look like a "piece of cake." And she and her husband had harsh words over the wisdom of her leaving her high paying job. He just didn't understand how difficult her life had become. He probably watched the Huxtables too.

In addition to these "supermoms" (still available in syndication), today viewers follow the antics of more controversial moms like Lois in *Malcolm in the Middle*, who appeared topless in one episode and disciplines her children with a "chop chop" and a whack upside the head. TV mom Roseanne, still popular in syndication, puts men down on a regular basis and is a general loudmouth. The scantily clad Peg Bundy on *Married with Children*, also in syndication, is a rotten housewife who doesn't cook or clean, but spends her days watching TV, gorging on chocolates and insulting her family. Again, what we know about the influence of TV tells us that many girls will grow up thinking this is how to be a mom and that many boys will think these are the kinds of moms and wives they will encounter. *Malcolm in the Middle* has received very positive reviews as a good family show. But if your children are watching this without your input, you may be putting them in harm's way.

For all of their problems, these moms are at least married and provide a somewhat stable home environment. Single mothers on TV offer other problems. For example, my study of soap operas analyzed the lifestyle of single mothers.[4] I found that these mothers are portrayed as having a solid education, lucrative and rewarding careers, active social lives and men in their lives who support and nurture the moms and their babies. These moms sacrifice very little to have children. For example, several of these mothers bring their babies with them to work. Overall, they lead very "cushy" lives. Compare this to the lifestyle of the real life unmarried mom. In real life, forty-five percent of single mothers and their children live in poverty.[5] Their kids generally encounter more emotional and crime problems, have lower IQ's and suffer from lifelong learning disabilities.

For example, single mother Melissa is an undergraduate at a large Midwestern university, majoring in communications with an eye toward a career in public relations. Her life as a single mom consists of school, working at McDonald's to pay her tuition bills and getting health care for her two-year-old daughter, who has unexplained seizures. A social life? Melissa laughs that she has no time. Melissa's lifestyle is quite a contrast to those single mothers on the soaps. And her life is a lot better than that of most single moms—at least she is able to get an education.

Following the study of the soap opera moms, I gave a survey about the lifestyles of real-life single mothers to middle school and high school students. The results showed that more soap opera viewers than non-soap opera viewers thought that being a single mom was a fairly easy task. The kids who watched the soaps believed the moms they saw on in these programs were realistic. Many of the kids said they had grown up with soap opera characters, regularly watching the soaps as toddlers, often while in day care. They felt that they knew these characters better than any other adults, and many felt they had an almost "real" relationship with them.

When my friend Diane, who works with single moms at a community college, heard about my study, she asked her students if they watched soap operas. Most of them did and had since they were preschoolers. Now, watching soaps surely didn't cause these young women to get pregnant, but the cumulative effect of perhaps eighteen years of relationships with TV characters surely has had an impact. The moms they saw on the soaps may have made them less concerned about the consequences of premarital sex than they would have been otherwise.

Fathers

Just as influential as TV moms, TV dads fall into two main categories. The fathers of the '80s, like Jason Seaver, the psychologist on *Growing Pains*, were "superdads." Although they had successful careers, they still could get away at a moment's notice to pick up a sick child from school or meet with a teacher about academic problems. Many of the shows with "superdads" are still around in syndication.

Currently popular, the other type of dad is the ineffectual dad, like Drew Pickles on Nickelodeon's *Rugrats*. Drew is intimidated and manipulated by his three-year-old daughter, Angelica. In one episode, Angelica refused to eat her broccoli. Drew tried to cajole her with, "Come on, Sugar Pie, it's good for you. Don't you want to grow up to be big and strong?" She shouted, "No!" Following a nasty verbal exchange, Drew sent Angelica to her room. On the way upstairs she threatened, "You'll be sorry!" Drew looked worried and asked his wife, Charlotte, "Do you think she was serious when she said, 'You'll be sorry?'" Charlotte reassured him and he vowed that he wasn't going to be pushed around by a preschooler. However, Drew dreamed that night that Angelica successfully sued her parents for mistreating her and was awarded the house and all of their assets. When he woke up, he went to check on Angelica and said, "Hi, Sweetie." Angelica replied, "I'm sorry I was a bad girl." He said, "No, honey, I'm the one who should be sorry. I shouldn't have tried to make you eat the broccoli. From now on, you can try the foods you're ready to try." Angelica: "Oh, Daddy, you're the greatest." Drew: "Sleep tight, Princess." Angelica then winked at the camera and said, "Heh, heh, it works every time."

As models for boys, both of these dad types are troublesome. Boys who think being a "superdad" is easy will find it much more difficult than it looks on television, and in terms of shaping viewers' expectations, girls who assume the man they marry will be like the "superdads" may well be disappointed with their husbands' inability to deliver. These superdads may also make kids think that their own dads are not competent, as well. Again, it is folly to assume that your children will figure this out on their own. Of course, incompetent fathers like Drew Pickles are undesirable as both models and shapers of expectations.

Unmarried TV dads have been portrayed just as unrealistically as unmarried moms. Since the 1950s, more families on television were headed by single dads than single moms, a situation not reinforced by real census figures.

During the decade of the 1950s, 17 percent of single heads of household on TV were dads, compared to just one percent of real-life single dads as heads of households.[6] *Bachelor Father* was one such show, premiering in 1957. John Forsythe played the foster father raising his niece, whose real parents were killed. The Forsythe character was a playboy type, learning how to be a good parent with the help of his Chinese houseboy. *My Three Sons*, also premiering in 1957, featured the widowed Steve Douglas raising his boys with the help of his also widowed father-in-law. Although Steve was a distant father, often featured working in his office, he was in control.

Throughout the 1960s, 28 percent of TV households were headed by single dads compared to just one percent in the real population.[7] In 1966, *Family Affair* came on the air, featuring an affluent engineer raising his orphaned nieces and nephew with the help of a butler. These children were "perfect" kids who didn't challenge authority or get into trouble. In 1969, *The Courtship of Eddie's Father* featured Eddie as a lonely child cared for by a Japanese maid. Eddie was preoccupied with finding a wife for his widowed father. In 1975, *Diff'rent Strokes* premiered, featuring a White millionaire who adopted two Black kids from the ghetto, an equally unrealistic situation.

More recently, between 1990 and 1995, 23 percent of television families were headed by single dads compared to just three and one-half percent in the real population.[8] Both *Party of Five* and *7th Heaven* are headed by oldest brothers in families with dead parents.

Real-life families with single dads bear little resemblance to these TV families. Jim O'Kane, a single dad with a real interest in single dads on TV, has a website that includes synopses of 130 TV shows that have featured single dads.[9] Virtually none of the TV dads had been divorced, but rather widowed, a situation that eliminates much of the conflict real families deal with concerning such things as which parent "gets" Christmas this year or when to send the kids to summer camp. Further, real-life single dads rarely have what O'Kane refers to as "stand-in moms"—the butler, nanny or housekeeper. Eric, a student at a large northern university, has been raised by his divorced single dad since he was twelve. A real challenge was dealing with his father's alcoholism, but after a few years of Alanon, AA and Alateen, his father recovered and life became better. As an only child, he described the "team" he and his father were and how their house was spotless because the two of them kept it that way, not because a housekeeper did it. Eric also noticed that kids in TV families were always getting into some kind of trouble and described the value his dad placed on getting good grades and staying out of trouble. Another difference between Eric's family and TV families is that on TV, families are generally affluent and can indulge their children. Because money was rather tight in Eric's family, he got a job in junior high so he would never have to ask his dad for money.

Parents

In general, TV's portrayal of parents offers problems. In many television families, the parents are not the chief decision makers. Rather, the children in the programs direct many family activities.[10] The Huxtable parents are the ones Dr. Brothers said real-life parents should imitate to be better parents. However, the Huxtable children, not the parents, are in charge and tell their siblings what to do.

For example, in one episode Rudy's school assignment was to get pictures of various animals. Since Cliff and Claire were unavailable, Vanessa suggested that, rather than draw the pictures, her little sister should look for pictures in magazines. When Claire was out of town, the extent of Cliff's directing the children was to suggest that Rudy write her mom a letter. But it was Vanessa who explained to Rudy how to actually write it.

Is there evidence of this abdication of parental roles in real life? A recent *The Oprah Show*[11] featured Craig and

Robyn Minnette, who appeared to be about 30 years old, and their five-year-old son, Dylan. They admitted that Dylan watches TV from the moment he gets up until he goes to bed at about 11:00 P.M. His mom serves him breakfast, lunch and dinner in front of the TV. He even has to have it on when he is in bed, sleeping, at night. If his parents turn it off after he is asleep and he wakes during the night, he "freaks out." They said they're afraid to limit his viewing because he will "freak out," and they "can't say 'no' to him."

Dylan also demands all of the things he sees advertised on TV, and his mom and dad buy the things because as two working parents they feel guilty about the little time they spend with him. They are also concerned about how they will enforce a reasonable bedtime next year when he goes to kindergarten. Meanwhile, they frequently ask themselves about what kind of social skills will he have when he gets there? What about how to be a friend with so little contact with other kids? Worse yet, what kind of kid will Dylan be at sixteen when he wants something like a sports car.

One example of television families dominated by children continues in Nickelodeon's *Rugrats*, in which the family is run by the tyrannical three-year-old Angelica Pickles. When five-year-old Ellen, a devotee of the *Rugrats*, doesn't get her way, she throws Angelica-style tantrums complete with furrowed eyebrows, sullen sneer, crossed arms and defiant stance. Ellen's mother has revealed Ellen knows that Angelica is mean and bad. Simply put, Ellen is imitating the Angelica behavior, even though she knows it's mean and bad. Interestingly, Ellen has a twin brother who does not act like Angelica. Why? Children tend to imitate characters that resemble themselves, and in this case Ellen is relating to the behavior of a girl. Her brother probably does not so readily identify with Angelica.

Siblings

Before I began my academic research concerning siblings on TV, I researched sibling relationships in real life. The sibling relationship is an extremely important one.[12] First of all, it is likely to be the longest lived relationship we have. We have siblings before we find a mate and after our parents die. Interactions with siblings teach us about interpersonal relationships—how to get along with others.

In healthy sibling relationships, children learn the ways of the world by observing older brothers and sisters. Unfortunately, very little of this mentoring occurs in current television programs.[13] However, 1950's sitcoms did show siblings supporting each other. In an episode of *Leave It to Beaver*, older brother Wally was in charge of a "Blind Date Committee" at school. Beaver asked Wally what this committee was all about, and Wally carefully explained that some girls and boys wanted to go to the school dance but were afraid to ask someone to go with them. The Blind Date Committee solved this problem by acting as matchmakers. Beaver had an "aha" response and learned something about the teenage world.

In 1980's and 1990's sitcoms, sibling interactions rarely dealt with helping younger brothers and sisters grow up.

One exception was Alex, the older brother on *Family Ties*. In one episode, Alex explained to his younger brother Andy that it was important to dress up and mind his manners when going to a restaurant because "Keaton men" were always polite and well-behaved in public. Unfortunately, this kind of coaching younger siblings in the ways of more grown up behavior is seldom seen in families on TV today.

Siblings are not only role models, but they provide each other with opportunities to try out new roles—if a younger sibling acts stupid, an older one offers feedback. In real life, kids need siblings to give them a way to try out new things such as new looks, personas and so on. But on television, siblings are often nasty in their feedback.

On *Growing Pains*, for example, Mike criticized a new dress of Carol's, saying nastily, "It might be okay in Bulgaria, but not here." Real-life siblings who use this type of television "script" create pain rather than safety.

In addition to being mentors and critics, siblings are also important as teachers of skills. In real life, a girl may teach her younger sister how to swim, or a big brother may give a younger one tips on how to get a girl's attention. This kind of direct teaching was sometimes shown on 1950's and 1960's TV.

On *The Brady Bunch*, for example, Peter got beaten up by Buddy Hinton for defending Cindy. Greg and the others convinced Peter to get revenge and taught him how to box. Peter was successful, knocking out Buddy's tooth. Though violence certainly wasn't the best way for Peter to solve his problem, the older siblings did teach the younger one a skill. However, few current TV siblings teach younger ones new skills of any kind. Parents and caregivers of children need to watch television with an eye toward what is omitted as well as what is included, and they should help kids analyze what is lacking in family relationships on TV.

Finally, siblings serve as a "bridge" for each other, breaking the way for younger siblings to deal with parents. In real life, Joan, age 24, Sally, age 20, and Shirley, age 16, are sisters. Joan and Sally were not allowed to date until they were 16 and had an 11:00 P.M. curfew. They complained bitterly and resisted the restrictions. While their whining and rebellion didn't pay off for them, Shirley has been going out with boys since she was 14 and has no curfew. On 1950's TV there were some examples of this bridging. On *Leave It to Beaver* Wally and the Beaver broke a garage window playing baseball. The Beaver was afraid of the punishment their dad would give them, but Wally said that he knew what to do. If they managed to fix it quick or at least try to fix it, their dad would go easy on them. The plan worked, and the Beaver learned a new strategy. Today, there are very few of these examples on TV.

To compare siblings of 1950's TV to those of 1980's TV, I conducted a study that analyzed every interaction between siblings, both verbal and nonverbal, such as sneers, smirks or gestures.[14] In the 1950s shows, *Ozzie and Harriet, Father Knows Best*, and *Leave It to Beaver*, 74 percent of the communication between siblings was positive. In contrast, in the 1980's shows of *Growing Pains, Family Ties*, and *The Cosby Show*, only 56 percent of the communication was positive. In other words, nearly half of the communication was negative.

During the 1990s, adult relationship shows such as *Seinfeld* and *Friends* replaced the family sitcom. Of the family sitcoms that remained, many sibling relationships were hostile. On *Roseanne* a conflict between Becky and Darlene ended with Becky telling Darlene, "God, I hate you! Just go to school." On *Married With Children* Kelly insulted her brother Bud, and he retorted by calling her a "beach blanket bimbo" and her and her friends "slut-kateers." Here, TV is telling viewers to expect conflict and derision from siblings.

Other family sitcoms, *The Wonder Years*, and *Home Improvement*, focused very little on the sibling relationship. In a remarkable break from the pattern, *The Simpsons* does focus on siblings, and 71 percent of the sibling communication has been positive.[15]

Studies of real-life brothers and sisters describe the sibling relationship as loyal and helpful in shaping one's self-identity, but television siblings do not offer many models of loyalty and helpfulness. Indeed, children who watch a lot of TV probably wouldn't see the prospect of a new sister or brother as a great thing at all and would learn to insult and discourage a new sibling.

Glenna and Her Nine TV Sets: Television and Family Interaction

Television has an enormous impact on family interaction. In fact, in many families the furniture is arranged around the television set. The TV is central to most households.

In the early days of television, families had just one black-and-white set. Choosing programs involved serious negotiation. In the 1950s, my sister and I were allowed to watch television for two hours per week, and we had to agree on what programs those would be. If anyone in the family wanted to watch television, it would be during those two hours, which resulted in the family being together during that time. Nowadays, most families have more than one television set, and two hours a *day* (not week) is seen as a reasonable limit. Glenna, who lives with her boyfriend and her ten-year-old daughter, has nine television sets in her home. Though Glenna's case may be rather extreme, clearly there is no need for the members of *that* household to negotiate about what is viewed or to view programming together.

Television also diverts time from activities that used to promote family interaction. Meals are rarely eaten together at a table, as they are in Homer and Marge Simpson's household. In real life, if meals are eaten as a family, the TV is frequently plays in the background. The addition to the TV lineup of *Teletubbies*, a program targeted at very young babies, makes it easier to avoid interaction with infants, the children who need the most attention of all. Peggy Charren of Action for Children's Television commented that there is something "very disconcerting" about a program for viewers who have to be propped up to watch it.[16]

Of course, television is used as a babysitter for kids of all ages on a routine basis. Maria and Walt brag that Saturday morning TV buys them two extra hours of sleep. They leave their kids' TV tuned in to Nickelodeon and tell the kids to wake them up when *SpongeBob SquarePants* is over, and not before then. They trust that their kids won't switch the channel to *Power Rangers*, but they haven't gotten up early to check it out.

For many families, television regulates many activities. Six-year-old Rick knows he should leave for the school bus when the second commercial break is over in *Pokemon*. Here, television is used to tell time. Thirty-year-old Sarah can't go to sleep until the ten o'clock news is over, even though she only watches it for the weather. Although she can see all the weather she wants on The Weather Channel, she says she "needs" to see it on the news. And Ann has given up trying to get her seven-year-old to bed before watching *Star Trek: The Next Generation*, even though it ends past his bedtime.

Furthermore, television is often used to avoid interaction altogether. In stressed families, it's often turned on so that people don't have to talk to each other. Joe and Lila say that when they were separated, their kids watched twice as much TV as when they were a happy couple. The kids figured that they could avoid getting into trouble with their mother, with whom they lived, if they didn't have to talk to her. And Ray confesses that he turns the TV on when his mother-in-law visits because she talks incessantly, and television is a way to avoid listening to her.

Television has also changed leisure time. In the early days of television with limited program schedules, adults bowled, went to movies, took dancing classes and visited with neighbors. Now, watching TV is the primary leisure activity for adults. The average American adult has 41 hours a week free for pleasure, and four times as much time is spent watching TV compared to any other activity.[17] And although many kids are programmed into a routine of such things as swimming classes, soccer practice and scout troop meetings, the average child spends close to three hours daily watching TV, and this doesn't include time spent with other media such as video games.[18]

—What You Can Do—

Sit down with your children and watch a family-based sitcom. Consider discussing the following:

- What does the mother in this program do? If you're watching a "supermom," point out the things they don't seem to do—the boring parts of real work and the dirty work of homemaking (cleaning bathrooms, for example). If you're watching a "mom" who you don't think is a good example of a mom—a raunchy mom like Lois of *Malcolm in the Middle* or a sarcastic mom like Roseanne or Peg Bundy—point out what you find objectionable and explain why. Explain that in real life these moms may not be anything like the TV mom they play.

- Try to find a show with a single mom and watch it with your children. Ask them to think about a family they know that is headed by a single mom. If they don't know such a family, tell them about some of the difficulties single moms face—reduced income, handling all of the parenting, etc. You don't want your children thinking that being a single mom is an easy task.

- Look at the fathers. What do you see them doing? If you're watching a "superdad," ask them what work-related things do the TV "dads" do? Are they ever shown doing the mundane tasks of real work? Do they do the "dad" jobs that real dads do—take out the garbage or feed the dog, for example? If you're watching a nincompoop who you find objectionable, point out the problems you see and explain why. Explain that the TV dads are reading from scripts and that in real life they might not be like the dad they play on TV.

- Try to find a show with a single dad and watch it together. Do you or your children know any family headed by a single dad? What would be the challenges in a real-life family headed by a single dad?

- Ask your children who's in charge in the family you are watching? How do decisions get made? Do the parents control what goes on? Or do the kids? Discuss who you think should make decisions and explain why.

- How do siblings get along in this TV family? Are they helpful and supportive? Or are they nasty? Do they put each other down? If you object to the way TV siblings act, discuss this with your children.

- Get rid of some of your TV sets. Seriously consider making do with just one set.

- Put your TV set in an out-of-the-way place. My mom put ours in the basement, which was dusty, dreary and dank. We had to really want to watch a program to go there.

- Put a limit on how much television your kids can watch.

- Put a limit on how much television you watch. Kids look to you as a role model, and if you watch a lot of TV, they will too.

- Watch the behaviors of you and your children as if you were an outsider watching your family. Do your family members resemble any of those you see on TV? Become self-conscious about how you act toward each other. Do you like what you see?

Chapter 2

Sex and the City, and the Burbs and the Boonies:

What the Media Teaches About Dating and Sex

Justine teaches Art in a suburb of a large Midwestern city. One of her third grade students sculpted two crude human figures, joined them erotically and told a pornographic story. Perhaps he had seen a pornographic magazine or movie on cable, although the boy's mother told Justine he surely didn't see this stuff when she was around. But he saw it somewhere—at a friend's house or perhaps on a TV set in his bedroom that his mother couldn't see.

While this story is disturbing enough, sexuality is creeping into the lives of even younger children. A preschool teacher in Massachusetts saw a four-year-old boy lying on top of a four-year-old girl during free-play time. When she asked what they were doing, they said they were having sex. In Manhattan, a young boy thought he was paying a girl a compliment by saying that he wanted to rape her.[1] A 10-year-old boy asked his teacher to explain oral sex, and his question was followed up by an eight-year-old girl's request that the teacher explain anal sex.[2] Suggestive toys like Mattel's "Baywatch Barbie" are marketed to children ages three and up. Is *Baywatch* really about being a lifeguard, as a Mattel executive claimed?[3]

Where do kids get these ideas? Beginning at a very young age, children learn about dating, love and sex from the media, especially television. The average adolescent is exposed to 15,000 sexual references on television per year.[4] In fact, 29 percent of teens report that TV is their most important source of information about sex.[5] These statistics are disturbing, given the nature of the portrayal of sex on television.

Dating on TV

In the 1980s and earlier, television programs, especially sitcoms, sometimes featured actual dating. On *The Cosby Show*, for example, Theo rehearsed a phone call to ask a girl for a date. To him, a date was important enough to be sure to say the right things. On *Family Ties*, Mallory introduced her date to her family. She also took dating seriously and wanted her family's approval of her boyfriend. This kind of traditional dating on TV is rare today. So kids who are getting their ideas about dating and relationships from TV are not getting the idea that dating and courtship should be taken seriously. Indeed, an examination of relationships on TV reveals the opposite case.

One source of information about dating comes from TV game shows. The website "Games for Singles" lists 23 dating game shows. Those that aren't in first run are generally in reruns and/or on the Game Show Network. On the 1960's pioneer singles show, *The Dating Game*, bachelorettes asked questions of three bachelors. The bachelors and bachelorette were hidden from each other by a screen. After asking several questions, often as irrelevant as "if you could be a car, what kind of car would you be?" the bachelorette chose a date based on the men's answers.

Compared to *The Dating Game*, the 1990s hit *Studs*, was rather raunchy. On it, two men went on dates with the same three women. Afterward the guys had to guess which woman said what about them. The roles were also reversed with two women going out with the same three men. The contestants' statements smoldered with sexual innuendo. "That girl was so hot, she could set the North Pole on fire!" "When I took her to McDonald's for dinner, even Ronald McDonald couldn't keep his eyes off of her!"[6]

Another recent show, MTV's *Singled Out* featured bachelors and bachelorettes rating desirable attributes for the opposite sex. Kummerer's 1998 study[7] of the show found that the desired traits of men included "bedroom behavior," "good butt," "kissing style," "underwear," as well as a few mundane categories, such as "career goals" and "lifestyle." In general, bachelorettes on the show focused on physical attributes 60 percent of the time. Bachelors chose attributes related to appearance 40 percent of the time. While men claimed that commitment was a desired trait 30 percent of the time, it was chosen so they could *eliminate* a woman who wanted commitment.

Chuck Woolery, a long time game show host and host of the dating game show *Love Connection*, commented on NPR's *Todd Mundt Show* that current dating shows are heavily into humiliating possible dates. He said that on these shows mean-spirited, hurtful and embarrassing comments are common.[8] He cited the dating show, *elimiDATE*, as an example. The show features one man (or woman, but usually a man) and four women (or men) as possible dates. All five start out on the date, with the four contestants vying for selection as "the date" for the evening. The competitors quickly become nasty. One woman accused another of having breast implants, and another of being an experienced lap dancer. One woman found a competitor so bitchy that she threw a drink in her face. Rivals refer to the competition as creeps, losers and poseurs.

Local television stations air reruns of many of these shows, frequently during the daytime when they attract young viewers. In many markets, *Studs* is aired at 3:00 P.M., and dating shows are also aired in the late morning. A new wrinkle capitalizes on the popularity of reality-based shows such as *Survivor. Mr. Personality*, hosted by Monica Lewinsky, features masked men vying for the attention of several women, all of them living in a mansion in Malibu. In one scene, Mindy offers to demonstrate to Brian how she is "better" than Hayley, on whom Brian had set his sights. Behind closed doors we hear a zipper sound followed by erotic moans. It's clear that whether or not oral sex actually occurred, viewers were supposed to infer that it did. This program is aired on a FOX TV Station at 8:00 P.M. in my time zone. The premise of *Temptation Island* is that four committed couples join with 26 singles and spend two weeks at an exotic location. The couples are separated and date the singles, supposedly to test the strength of their relationships. Another new reality dating show was a seven-part series, *Joe Millionaire;* a bachelor posing as a millionaire courts 20 girls in a luxurious location in France. Joe, who is really a construction worker earning $19,000 a year claims to have inherited $50 million. He courts the women, eliminating them over the course of the series until one remains. Then he reveals that he is not a millionaire and comes clean. Then, we learn whether or not his choice will have him, now knowing the truth.

What kids see on game shows is that kind of object you'd like to be (e.g., like a car); steamy sexuality and appearance are extremely important. Traits such as personality, education and goals are much less important in finding a good dating match. Unless kids are watching 1980's reruns of sitcoms they are not likely to see any images of what we might call "traditional" dating. Few, if any, of these programs offer constructive ideas about dating.

Sex in Prime Time TV

During the 1999–2000 television season, the Kaiser Family Foundation conducted a study of sex on TV and found that more than two-thirds of all programs contain sexual content (talk about sex as well as sexual behaviors).[9] Sexual content occurred in 89 percent of all movies aired on television. Eighty-four percent of sitcoms contained sexual references or activities, second only to movies. Not even soap operas had as much sexual content as sitcoms. Compare these figures to the 1997–1998 season when "only" 56 percent of sitcoms contained sexual content. Parents whose ideas about sitcom content are based on their own sitcom viewing of just a few years ago need to spend some time watching the current sitcoms. They may be startled to see what is aired during the so-called "family hour." The "family hour" no longer exists.

Sex Talk

The Kaiser study found that in sitcoms, most of the sexual content involved talking about sex. On *Dawson's Creek*, for example, a program targeted at adolescent and adult viewers (but enjoyed by many preadolescents), the characters rarely talk about anything except sex. Although many of the characters advocate keeping one's virginity, the teens describe their parents' intimacies, ponder aloud whether they themselves are ready for sex and gossip about who is having sex with whom. One reviewer noted that "nobody is interested in hobbies, learning, sports, politics, religion, social life or any kind of work unless it involves movies or TV."[10]

Other talk is more explicit. In one episode of *Friends*, a show wildly popular with middle school students, Chandler burst into his apartment with the words: "I had sex two hours ago!" A short while later, the woman with whom he had sex phoned. Though she thinks she's talking to someone else, she's actually talking to Chandler—and she describes the sex as "bumpy" and so quick she wasn't satisfied. An even more graphic show is *Sex and the City*, a popular and award-winning program on HBO airing at 8:00 P.M. in the Central Time Zone, a time when it's easily available to young viewers. In one episode, Samantha told her friends that she loved Dick's dick. "It's long, pink, perfect. It's dickalicious!" Other prime time shows, such as *Caroline in the City* and *Melrose Place*, contain explicit talk or innuendoes about such topics as penis size, having sex with strangers and being successful at getting a guy to have sex with you by assuring him that you want no commitment. Ward's study[11] of talk about sex in prime time concluded that on TV men regard sex as a competition—who can "score" with the most women. The women on TV account for much less sexual talk compared to men, and their sexual talk focuses on the attractiveness of men's bodies. Both men and women regard sex as a recreational activity that doesn't require a long-term relationship.

Sexual Behaviors

Many programs contain not just sexual talk but also sexual activity. The Kaiser study[12] of 1,100 randomly selected programs in all genres except news found that 27 percent of the programs contained actual sexual behaviors, ranging from physical flirting to real or implied intercourse. In one episode of *Sex and the City*, Samantha asked her date to "show [her his] dick." He dropped his pants, and viewers saw his penis—frontal nudity in prime time! In another episode, Miranda went on a blind date with a "hot guy" and at the end of that first date he fondled her breasts. At the time she was pregnant with another man's baby, and she asked Carrie if it was okay to have sex with a guy when you're pregnant with someone else's child!

On an episode of *Felicity*, her boyfriend's dad came to

visit her hoping she could help him reconcile with his son, who had rejected him because of his alcoholism. When the dad burst into tears, Felicity gave him a hug to comfort him, and he began kissing her neck as he made his way to her mouth. And on *Dawson's Creek*, Pacey was working at a video store when his English teacher came in wearing very seductive, almost lingerie-styled clothing—and flirted with him.

Sexual Intercourse

The Kaiser study also counted instances in which actual sexual intercourse was either shown or strongly suggested, and it found that 10 percent of the 1,100 programs sampled included intercourse. Only half of the couples who engaged in it had an established relationship.[13] The other half of the couples were those who knew each other and/or who had only just met. A controversial example of intercourse occurred on *Dawson's Creek*. During the first season, 15-year-old Pacey seduced and had sex with his English teacher. In real life, if a student tried to get a teacher into bed he would probably be rebuffed. But Tamara, the English teacher, encouraged Pacey—and they had sex.

In an episode of *Sex and the City*, Richard told Samantha to "get that perfect ass" into the shower with him, and she had an orgasm using the shower nozzle. In another episode, Miranda had sex with her lover, crying, "Fuck me! Fuck me like there's no tomorrow!"

Although the network sitcom *Friends* isn't quite as explicit as cable shows like *Sex in the City*, intercourse often is either displayed or implied. On Joey's second date with Kathy, he took her back to his apartment. Within moments he came out of the bedroom, dressed only in a towel. He sent his roommates out, explaining that although he and Kathy didn't plan on sleeping, they needed privacy in the bedroom. On *Ally McBeal*, Ally had sex with a stranger in a car wash. And in an episode of *Felicity*, Felicity had sex with Eli because she was peeved at her boyfriend, Noel, and used this one-night stand to feel better. On TV shows like these, dating usually means sex, and sex is often casual.

Homosexuality in Prime Time

The portrayals of gay and lesbian characters in prime-time television have surely improved since the 1970s when Archie Bunker and others referred to them as "fags" and "fairies." But it wasn't until 1994 that a prime time series featured a gay character. The brief run of *My So-Called Life* featured a flamboyantly gay character, Rickie Vasquez. Since then more gay characters have appeared. *Dawson's Creek's* Jack McPhee, struggling with his homosexuality, came out to his friends and parents, and received support from them. In one episode that sparked controversy, Jack and his lover, Tobey, engaged in a five and one-half second on-screen kiss. *Will & Grace* includes two gay men, Will a successful lawyer whose mannerisms could easily be construed as "straight" and Jack, a stereotypical "campy" gay character. In the now-defunct program, *Ellen*, Ellen came out in an episode that garnered huge ratings. One year later it was canceled. Some said it was too "gay-specific" and that too much of the program dealt explicitly with gay issues.[14] *Queer as Folk* is a blatantly sexual program on Showtime. While gay issues, such as coming out to friends and parents, staying semi-closeted in the workplace and interpersonal relationships, are addressed, its primary focus is gay sex. In the opening scenes a narrator says, "The thing you need to know is, it's all about sex." It features nudity, explicit sex, and coarse language and characters often engage in anonymous anal sex in the gay discotheque, Babylon.

Responses to these programs have been mixed. Conservative groups such as the Alliance for Traditional Marriage and Values have expressed outrage at the portrayal of homosexuality on *Dawson's Creek,* and claim that it is an outright attempt to promote homosexuality.[15] Another critique claimed that it misleads viewers into thinking that "'homosexuality is something you're born with.'"[16]

On the other hand, liberal groups praise the portrayal of gay characters and the fact that the gayness of the characters is part of an integrated storyline. The characters are portrayed as three-dimensional men and women, not just gay people. Liberal groups also note that the presence of homosexual characters is important, inasmuch as there are gays in the real world. They point to the hostility that many gay teens must live with. A nationwide survey conducted by the Gay, Lesbian, and Straight Education Network found that 69 percent of gay adolescents have been the target of verbal, physical or sexual harassment in the school setting. Moreover, 42 percent reported that they had been physically attacked.[17] Taunting and harassment result in feelings of alienation and isolation. For many homosexual teens, the lack of representation of gays on TV reinforces their feelings of isolation. This often creates agony in young people; indeed, researchers report that gay teens are five times as likely to attempt suicide than heterosexual teens,[18] and three times more likely to successfully commit suicide than heterosexual teens.[19]

During the 2001–2002 season, 20 lesbian and gay characters appeared on network television. Their presence could help gay adolescents feel less isolated and give them a sense of validation in the world. However, in the 2002–2003 season, 11 shows featuring gay and lesbian characters did not return. This decline in a gay presence leads to what some researchers call "symbolic annihilation," the notion that because there are no characters that a homosexual youth can relate to, he or she may as well be dead.[20] In addition to the limited presence of gay characters, the irresponsible sexual behavior of the characters on *Queer as Folk* can be argued to have a negative impact on gay teen viewers.

So we see that on prime time television, heterosexual

talk and behaviors are rampant. We also see that homosexual characters and homosexual behaviors have not made serious inroads into prime time television. Further both heterosexual and homosexual characters are largely sexually irresponsible, providing very risky models to young viewers.

Sex on Soap Operas

Another source of sexual content is the daytime soap opera. Eighty percent of soap operas contain sexual content, much of it involving intercourse. One study of 50 hours of soap operas found 156 acts of actual intercourse.[21] Even more troubling, 94 percent of the sexual encounters on the soaps are between unmarried partners.[22] Much of the intercourse involves uncommitted partners, and characters commonly have multiple partners.

On *The Young and the Restless*, Nick and Sharon were a married couple who owned a coffeehouse called Crimson Lights. Diego was hired as a waiter and Sharon began confiding in him about the miscarriage she had that she blamed on Nick. Soon, Sharon had a one night stand with Diego. Then Nick's sister, Victoria, fell in love with Diego, and when she learned about the one night stand, she told her brother (Sharon's husband). For revenge, Nick slept with Grace, who had previously tried to break up Nick and Sharon's marriage. Even marriage is rarely seen as a highly committed relationship.

On *The Bold and the Beautiful*, Brooke married Eric long ago and had two children, Rick and Bridget, who are now grown up. Later, Brooke married Eric's son, Ridge and, afterward, Thorne. Recently, Bridget married Deacon, with whom she was deeply in love. Deacon was not as deeply in love with her because he had sex with her mother, Brooke, while he and Bridget were married. Brooke got pregnant with Deacon's child, and, to hide this fact from Bridget, married Whip and told everyone that the baby was his. But Bridget learned that Deacon was the real father, and she ended her relationship with Deacon. Ex-spouses abound and often have sex with not only their current spouses, but also their ex-spouses.

On the soaps, single motherhood is rampant but not difficult. Perhaps most disturbing of all, while intercourse between multiple partners is prevalent, safe sex is rarely practiced. In the study that found 156 acts of sexual intercourse, there were only five references to contraception or safe sex.

Some parents may believe they don't have to worry about soap opera content because they think kids don't watch these shows. But the junior and senior high students in my survey of soap opera viewing reported that the students' moms routinely taped their favorite soaps so the students could watch them after school or in marathon viewings on the weekends. Indeed, many of these students said they had been watching the soaps for as long as they could remember and felt closer to some soap opera characters than to their own relatives.

Safe Sex

TV rarely portrays safe sex, and the consequences of sex are often unexplored or unrealistic. Of the 15,000 sexual references kids see per year, less than 10 percent of them have anything to do with safe sex.[23] While 84 percent of sitcoms contain sexual content, only 5 percent mention either safe sex or the possible consequences of sexual intercourse,[24] and only 3 percent of soaps refer to safe sex.[25] In real life, there are 900,000 teen pregnancies each year,[26] and incidents of sexually transmitted diseases are increasing. For example, a study reported in 2002 that nearly half of sexually active girls between 15 and 19 years old contracted the virus that leads to genital warts within three years of losing their virginity.[27]

Talk Shows

Sexual references abound on daytime talk shows. *The Jerry Springer Show,* rated by TV Guide in 2002 as the worst show in the history of television,[28] airs twice each weekday in many markets. Jerry features guests such as Jon, who's having an affair with Kim who reveals that she's really a man; and Monique, who learns that her lover, Cedric, has been sleeping with her sister. *Sally Jessie Raphael* and *Jenny Jones,* others nearly as sleazy and exploitative, were aired twice daily, and at least one airing was late enough in the afternoon that kids could watch. Take, for instance, *Maury;* there 21-year-old Brandon described how he had seven children with six different women. Another *Maury* guest, Cindy, didn't know which of six men was the father of her daughter. An episode of *Sally* featured 13- to 16-year-old girls who proudly described their unprotected sex. Valerie first had sex at age 12 and has had 15 partners. She never used protection, because it "[didn't] feel right."[29] In 1995, a *Jenny Jones* program featured secret admirers and their crushes. Scott Amedure admitted that he had a crush on Jon Schmitz and described in detail a sexual fantasy he had about Schmitz. Schmitz had the impression that the secret admirer was a woman and was so humiliated by the revelation and the sexual fantasy that he shot and killed Amedure.

Howard Stern is another sleazy talk show host. He has both a morning drive time radio and a late evening TV talk show. He conducts humiliating interviews and dares people to do tasteless and sexually oriented acts. During Breast Cancer Awareness Month, on his radio show, he performed a breast exam on a woman complete with commentary on her breasts' size and shape. He makes sexist and racist comments, makes fun of the handicapped and homeless, and routinely discusses masturbation, sexual intercourse, sex organs and homosexuality. On his TV show he routinely gets women to take off their clothes. Young viewers can easily watch this program because it is aired on E!

A possible beacon of hope among the trashy talk shows is *Loveline*, a call-in program featuring Dr. Drew Pinsky. It first aired on MTV and now is heard on the radio Sundays through Thursdays from 10:00 P.M. until midnight. As a practicing physician, Pinsky noticed that teens were getting very little sex education from their parents or other authority figures, and he believed there was a real need for teens to get accurate information.

On Dr. Pinsky's program, teens ask very candid questions: "Does the size of one's penis really matter to have good sex?" "How do I know if I have genital warts?" "Where can I get emergency contraception?" In addition to the show, Dr. Drew launched his own website, where visitors can pose questions and participate in chat rooms. Various topics are presented, related not only to sex but to general health issues—sexual abuse and drug abuse, for example. He also sends free condoms to any visitor who registers on the website.

This show is a "*possible* beacon of hope" because, although it is important that teens get accurate sexual information, it can also be argued that a show like this contributes to the epidemic of casual sex seen among teens.

Do Kids Pay Attention?

Evidence strongly suggests that kids do pay attention to and learn about sex from the media. One survey[30] found that nearly three out of four teens think TV affects the sexual behavior of their peers. Alarmingly, 29 percent of adolescent boys rated pornographic movies as their most important source of sex education.[31] A 1998 article in *Time* reported an interview with a 16-year-old girl who has slept with five guys. She said you can learn a lot about sex from TV, especially cable. "It's all mad-sex stuff." In the same article, a 14-year-old boy said that you can learn anything you want to know about sex from TV. You just have to channel surf, and you'll find out what you need to know. He learned to kiss from TV when he was eight, and the girl he kissed said he sure knew how to do it.[32]

These statements illustrate the importance of the notion that the media offer models that viewers often use for imitation. Many models of casual sexual behavior are likely to be imitated by viewers. For example, teens who see that Joey and Kathy have sex on the second date may well have sex on the second date themselves. In addition, we know that television shapes viewers' expectations about what will happen in the real world. This means that teens watching Miranda allow someone to fondle her breasts on the first date, and a blind date at that, might assume that this is appropriate behavior. Indeed, the widespread casual sex on TV contributes to what teen viewers think is "normal."

There is ample evidence that the type of casual sex presented in the media does exist in real life, especially among teenagers. According to Shoshana, a 17-year-old girl from New Jersey, girls at her school feel perfectly comfortable giving oral sex to boys they have just met at a party. Kara, an Illinois teenager, said that she and her friends lost their virginity at 14. They think it's important to have sex with a bunch of people to try them out. Other girls at her school frequently "hook up" with guys they've just met. At 18-year-old Amanda's Indiana high school, lots of kids have sex and want to experiment with different people. Amanda said that in the basement of one guy's house, kids do drugs and have group sex at regular orgies. She added that most people don't have sex until they have been dating for "at least two weeks."[33] Seventeen-year-old Tracy, from Philadelphi, lost her virginity at 14 and since has had seven different partners. Carla, a 15-year-old from San Francisco, has had at least 15 partners.[34]

Boys also believe in casual sex. A study of high school males reported that 75 percent of them, age 15–19, have had sexual intercourse[35] and thought that 13 different sexual partners before marriage was acceptable.[36] Another study found that 65 percent of boys think that it's okay for a male to force a female to have sex after six months of dating.[37]

This nonchalant attitude appears to be widespread in the United States. By the time students are seniors in high school, 70 percent have had sexual intercourse and 27 percent have had sex with four or more partners.[38] This behavior carries high risks.

There are nearly one million teen pregnancies each year and 40 percent of girls will become pregnant at least once before they reach age twenty.[39] The Centers for Disease Control and Prevention reports that sexually transmitted diseases and "anything but intercourse" (e.g., oral and anal sex) behaviors are rampant. Gonorrhea rates are higher in girls age 15–19 than any other age group. Several surveys report that as many as half of teens age 13–19 have had oral sex, and a physician in Chicago reported that girls often come to her clinic thinking they have strep when they have gonorrhea of the throat.[40]

This casual attitude about sex has also created an attitude of "entitlement" in boys. They think that after a couple of dates they deserve sex. A girl interviewed in *Time* said, "The guy will ask you up front. If you turn him down, you're a bitch . . . The guys are after us all the time, in the halls, everywhere."[41]

Is the sexual information offered by television counteracted by any other sources? Not very often. A survey of teens age 15–17 showed that half of them have never had a talk with their parents about when one is ready for sex.[42] One boy said his parents brought up sex when he was 13, but he had already learned everything from an older cousin.[43]

Just half of teens have asked their parents how to talk about sex with someone they are dating.[44] Young people also aren't talking with their sex partners about HIV/AIDS, other sexually transmitted diseases or birth control, and less than half have ever talked about birth control or STDs with a doctor or nurse.[45]

The bottom line, then, is that television and movies are the sources of information about sex for our children and adolescents. The messages they send are that unprotected casual sex is the norm and that there are rarely any negative consequences to this behavior. Given the statistics discussed earlier about the high incidence of teen pregnancies and the increasing incidents of STDs, this is a dangerous situation.

The absence of information from credible adults, as well as the heavy doses of sex on television, indicates that TV serves as a sex educator for many kids. Kids see an average of 15,000 sexual messages in a year on television. Less than 10 percent of those messages talk about safe sex or the risks of pregnancy. European kids also see a lot of sexual content on TV. But in the United States the rates of pregnancy, birth, abortion and STDs are many times higher than they are in Europe. A big difference is this: In European countries, widespread government supported public education programs address these issues, unimpeded by political and religious groups.[46]

The United States has the highest teen pregnancy rate in the western world![47] In addition to alarmingly high pregnancy rates, a study of 18- to 24-year-olds found a disturbing trend toward promiscuity, as indicated by multiple sex partners. In one study respondents indicated that in the *year* prior to the study, 24 percent had two to four partners and 9 percent had five or more partners. Since the age of 18, 15 percent had 5–10 partners, 8 percent had 10–20 partners, and 3 percent had *21 or more* partners![48]

—What You Can Do—

- Perhaps you were raised in a family that didn't talk about sexual matters. If so, you may be without a "script" to use to talk to your kids. If that's the case, educate yourself. There are many books available at your library or from an online bookseller. A number of them are listed in the appendix of this book. An advantage to the online booksellers is that they include customer reviews. Some books simply present information, and others take a moral stance of abstinence before marriage.

- Watch TV with your children. As sex is presented in the program (as it surely will be, especially if you're watching a sitcom), talk to them about whether this behavior is appropriate, safe and ethical. You also must watch the shows your children like and determine whether or not the sexual messages are ones that are appropriate for them.

- Recognize that sex education begins when your children are very young. It starts with how you talk about their bodies even as you change their diapers. Use the correct terms for body parts. If it embarrasses you to say "penis" or "vagina," begin using those terms at birth so that you can get past the embarrassment. By the time your children are seven or eight they should know what all the body parts are used for.

- Determine what your idea of "sexual integrity" is. Many parents believe that sex outside of marriage is wrong. Those parents must make their ethics and moral values clear to their children. Parents who condone sexual intercourse before marriage need to tackle the issue of promiscuity and casual sex. You must help your child make responsible sexual decisions.

- Remember that if you haven't had the sex talk by age 10, you have probably missed the chance to be the source of sexual information for your child.

- Parents who advocate abstinence, as well as those who condone sexual intercourse before marriage, must make their children aware of the possible consequences of sexual intercourse. Obviously, pregnancy is but one possible outcome. You must present your child with what the reality of an unplanned pregnancy would involve. The risk of acquiring a sexually transmitted disease (STD) is another. What would your child do if he or she thought she had an STD?

- You must also talk about the emotional consequences of having sexual intercourse before marriage. It often results in feelings of guilt or of "being cheap," especially for girls. Girls also risk getting a reputation of being "easy."

- Offer your kids strategies for resisting sexual pressure. You may want to role play various "scripts" for doing this. Accept the fact that, ultimately, your kids decide when to have sex.

- Be prepared to tell them about birth control so that if they do have sex, it won't be unprotected sex. Many parents fear that giving their child information about safer sex will only serve to encourage them to become sexually active. There is no evidence that this is the case.

- Recognize that you can't depend on the schools to adequately educate your children about sex. The quality of sex education varies widely from place to place, and you have no guarantee that the sex education program at your school will mesh with your attitudes about sex. Further, sex education usually deals with only the physical aspects of sex and does not address the emotional issues.

Talking openly with your kids might feel awkward, but the alternative is to let them learn their sexual mores and values from TV, pornography and peers. Is that a risk you want to take?

Chapter 3

"Don't Try This At Home!"

The Media, Violence and Aggression

At the age of 12, Lionel Tate killed his six-year-old friend, Tiffany, by imitating moves he'd seen on the *World Wrestling Federation TV Show*. An autopsy showed that Tiffany suffered from internal bleeding, a lacerated liver, fractured skull and a broken rib. The judge found Tate guilty of first-degree murder and sentenced him to life in prison without parole.[1] On one episode of MTV's *Jackass*, Johnny Knoxville hung steaks over his fire-resistant suit and then laid over a burning barbecue. Others in the cast poured lighter fluid on the coals and fanned the flames. Thirteen-year-old Jason Lind and a friend imitated the stunt, only without the flame-resistant suit. Jason was hospitalized in critical condition with second- and third-degree burns.[2]

Are these isolated events? They may be extreme, but they are not isolated. More than 3,500 scientific studies have looked at the relationship between media violence and violent behavior. Only 18 of those studies failed to find a relationship between the two. In fact, the relationship is stronger than that between smoking and lung cancer.[3] An important theory of media effects explains that many viewers tend to imitate behaviors they see on TV. Viewers are especially inclined to imitate violent behaviors if the TV characters don't get punished. The acts might not be imitated right away—viewers may store the behaviors they see as "behavioral scripts" that they can use at a later time, when they run into a situation that resembles the one they saw on TV.

One of the most persuasive of these 3,500 studies was conducted by a professor at the University of British Columbia, Tannis Willams. She learned about a town located in a remote valley that had no access to television. In 1973 the town made a deal with the Canadian Broadcasting Company to install a special transmitter for the town. Williams thought this would be an ideal happenstance for studying TV's impact on people and communities. Before television arrived, Williams and a team of researchers extensively examined community life. They studied such things as leisure time activities, reading fluency and aggression. Two years after television arrived, the team went back to this town, which they had dubbed NOTEL (for "no television"), and studied the same things. The biggest change was in the level of aggression. Aggressive behavior increased in all age groups of children, in both boys and girls, in children rated as both high and low aggressive before the study, and in both heavy and light viewers. The researchers also studied two similar towns that did have television. Over the same two-year period they found some increases in aggression, but nowhere near the increases of NOTEL.[4]

Does any evidence contradict the link between watching violence on TV and violent behavior? Occasionally someone claims that watching violence is therapeutic—that it helps get rid of violent tendencies—but none of the claims have been supported by research. The 3,500 studies mentioned above have been carefully examined by such highly respected organizations as the American Academy of Pediatrics, the American Medical Association, the American Psychological Association and the American Academy of

Child and Adolescent Psychiatry. These groups issued a joint statement to Congress in which they flatly stated that "watching violent entertainment can lead to increases in aggressive attitudes, values and behavior, particularly in children."[5]

How pervasive is violence on TV? A study reported in 1998 concluded that kids have seen, on average, 8,000 murders and 100,000 other violent acts by the time they finish grammar school.[6] Since that report, another study found that violence increased 78 percent between the 1998–1999 TV season and the 2000–2001 season,[7] so kids presently see even more murders and violent acts.

Violence in Children's Programming

Many parents worry about the physical violence on television, and there is plenty to worry about. In fact, you may be distressed to know that children's programming contains more violence than any other type of programming.[8] What kinds of programs are the sources of physical violence?

Cartoons and Animated Films

Cartoons and animated movies feature enormous amounts of violence. In fact, children see an average of 25 to 30 acts of violence in one hour of cartoons. This compares to three to five violent acts in prime time.[9] In one classic *Roadrunner* cartoon, Wile E. Coyote tries to catch the roadrunner using grenades, bombs, dynamite and knives. Although the bombs and grenades backfired and exploded on the coyote, he suffered only momentary injuries. More recently, *The Mighty Morphin Power Rangers,* in their mission to overcome evil, punch and kick the enemies but generally must use their "super gun" to win. They never show reluctance to engage in brutal combat. The Cartoon Network's extremely popular show, *The Power Puff Girls* brags that it features "grrl power." Day after day, these animated five-year-old sisters save their town from evil-doers by hitting them, punching them, burning them to a crisp and fracturing skulls. The characters in the relatively new, fast-action Japanese-style animation, such as *Pokemon, Digimon* and *Dragon Ball Z*, beat people to death, disintegrate bodies and smash people into rocks, killing them. They are aired on FOX Television Stations, WB and the Cartoon Network, often in marathon airings on Saturday mornings.[10]

Animated movies pose equal dangers. A study of all American animated movies produced between 1937 and 1999 found that all of them, (100 percent) included violence.[11] Every Disney movie features violence, and many of them have very dark sides.[12] In *Beauty and the Beast*, the beast is not only grotesque to look at, he is frightening and threatening before being tamed by Belle. Characters in this movie slap, hit, stab, shoot and scuffle with other characters, and wolves stalk Belle and her father. Snow White's evil stepmother sends Snow White into the woods with a huntsman who has orders to kill her and bring back her heart. *The Three Musketeers* impale their enemies on spikes, and the killing is done with glee. In spite of this, one grandmother told me it was easy for her to care for her five-year-old granddaughter for several days: "I just turn on the Cartoon Network." Many parents and grandparents assume that because it's animated it's safe. But just because it's animated doesn't mean that kids will know that it's not real. Children do not clearly distinguish between reality and fantasy until approximately age eight.[13]

Violence in TV Commercials in Children's Programming

In a class I taught about the media and children, we sampled some Saturday morning programming for children. The students and I noticed that, programs aside, the commercials featured a lot of violence. So I did a study of the violence and aggression in television commercials that featured child characters and aired during TV-Y and TV-Y7 programs.[14] I was concerned with the amount and kind of aggression there was in commercials in programs deemed "safe" for the very youngest viewers. I learned that more than one-third of the commercials had some kind of aggression or violence. The kids deface buildings, destroy objects and people in video games, twist arms and insult each other. Alarmingly, the most common kind of violence was what I called "fortuitous aggression"—aggression that comes out of the blue, unprovoked, and not caused by a character. For example, children performed on stage and during the performance their heads exploded. In another, a giant Cheerio bonked a kid on the head.

Music Videos and Song Lyrics

A recent analysis of music videos concluded that more than half of the concept videos (those that tell a story, rather than a concert video) feature violence.[15] Consider the lyrics from one of Eminem's Grammy and MTV music award winning albums, *Kill You*.[16] His lyrics talk about choking, sodomizing and raping one's mother. He also refers to *The Texas Chain Saw Massacre* and describes the image of brains dripping out of a victim's head.

The cover for Andrew W. K.'s album, *I Get Wet*, shows a picture of him with blood running down his face. He said he wanted it to be real blood so he took a cinder block and smashed his nose. In the lyrics from a song on his album, *Ready to Die*, he threatens to kill and tells a victim to prepare for his big judgment day and to die.[17]

In addition to the large doses of violence in music videos and song lyrics, the perpetrators rarely create serious injury or get punished. More than three-fourths of the violent acts in music videos result in no physical harm. In one video a man is beheaded and his head magically reattaches itself. Almost all of the violence is portrayed as right or justified, and more than half of it is committed by the "good guys."[18]

Professional Wrestling

Professional wrestling on cable and Pay Per View television provides viewers a heavy dose of violence and, currently, wrestling programs are the most popular programs on cable. Although the matches of the World Wrestling Federation (WWF), the World Championship Wrestling (WCW) and the Extreme Championship Wrestling (ECW) are rated TV-14, many viewers are much younger than 14. Indeed, many very young children attend the live matches. The kids often are not aware that most of the match is a well-choreographed show.

A reporter in Texas described how young children at a live match were upset, some even sobbing, at an interchange between a male and female wrestler. What was obviously a staged argument escalated into a fight in which the male physically attacked the woman; but, in the end, she managed to beat him up.[19] In another match, a male wrestler fighting a female held her upside down and then dropped her on her head. In real life, she surely would have broken her neck.[20] The online site for "Backyard Wrestling Videos" describes one that includes wrestlers fighting while engulfed in flames, a body slam off a four-story building, dives onto tables covered with thumbtacks, baseball bats slamming into groins and a fight on top of a car moving at 60 miles per hour.[21]

Slasher Films

Slasher films, also called "splatter" films, feature gory and grotesque violence. The villains dismember victims, behead them, cut out their hearts, burn them alive, and use pick axes, knives, drills, hammers and chainsaws as weapons. The films often associate killing with sex; before being assaulted, women frequently take off their clothes, masturbate or have sexual intercourse.

Women are more often victims in slasher films compared to other types of films, and they are shown terrified, trembling and begging for mercy. A study of 30 slasher films from the 1980s found that women were shown in fear and terror five times longer than male victims.[22] One of the earliest slasher films was the 1974 movie, *The Texas Chainsaw Massacre*. The villain wore a leather mask made out of people's skin. He killed people with a hammer and a chainsaw, and lived with a group of cannibals. In *Halloween*, generally thought of as the mother of all slasher films, Michael Myers watched his sister and her boyfriend cuddle and get ready to have sex. The boyfriend left the naked girl in the bedroom and Michael stabbed his sister to death. Fifteen years later, Michael escaped from a mental institution, exhumed his sister's body from her grave and "killed" her again on Halloween night. *Friday the 13th*, released in 1980, took place at a summer camp. In the 1950s a camper drowned while the counselors in charge were off somewhere having sex. Later, to avenge the drowning, counselors getting the camp ready to open for the season were killed off one by one. Freddy Krueger, in *A Nightmare on Elm Street* (1984), had a face with burnt skin and wore a glove with blades for fingers. He haunted four teenage girls in their dreams, chasing them endlessly, trying to slash them with his knived gloves. He slashed one girl to death after she had sex with her boy-friend. Even though the 1996 *Scream* was a parody of slasher films, the violence in it was gruesome and ugly. The parody doesn't eliminate the horror of the masked killer in a black tunic killing people and gutting them.

Although these movies are "R" rated, they are clearly targeted to the impressionable adolescent audience. Both boys and girls may come to think that being victimized is acceptable and perhaps even sexy. They are also likely to become desensitized to violence and gore, so that real-life violence doesn't bother them.

Television News

Because we tend to think of the news as "educational" we often don't think about the violence. However, news is aired for one thing and one thing only—to get viewers to watch the commercials, just like any other show. And broad-casters have found that violence attracts viewers. Indeed, a cliché in the broadcast news business is: "If it bleeds, it leads." The cliché was confirmed in a 1997 study that con-cluded that 43 percent of the news stories concerned violence or natural disasters.[23]

Verbal Violence

Must an act result in physical harm to be called aggres-sive or violent? I don't think so. In my research on television commercials featured in kids' programming, I looked at several types of aggression. One type of aggression I called verbal aggression, such as malicious teasing and insults. I included this type of aggression because we all know that the old adage "sticks and stones may break my bones, but words will never hurt me" is simply not true. I found that nearly one-third of the commercials included some type of aggression, some of it verbal.[24] Another recent study concluded that "coarse language," which was equated with "verbal violence," increased 78 percent between the 1998–1999 and the 2000–2001 television seasons.[25] During the so-called family hour, words such as "ass," "bitch," "bastard," "suck," "piss," "son of a bitch," "freaking" and "frigging" have become common.[26] In fact, when Bono accepted his Golden Globe Award in January of 2003, he said, "This is really, really fucking brilliant."[27] The word was not bleeped out. The show was aired at 7:00 P.M. central time. Surely many kids were watching it. Amazingly, very few viewers registered a complaint.[28]

Popular music is loaded with offensive language. I ask my college students to produce a musical biography, and a requirement is that the language of the narration as well as the lyrics of the songs must be "airable and in good taste"—language that would not offend their grandmothers. Students told me that I had given them an impossible assignment—that anything that was popular would offend their grandmothers.

What are the Effects of the Violence?

There are three effects we need to be concerned about with regard to watching a lot of violent media. One is that viewers behave more violently; another is that they become desensitized to it; and, further, they develop a fear of the world around them.

Increases in Violent Behavior

As mentioned earlier, thousands of studies have shown a relationship between watching a lot of violent TV and real-life violence. Preschool children who watch violent shows several times a week fight with playmates, destroy property and sass authority figures much more often than children who watch less-violent TV.[29] Cartoon violence carries with it particular risks. In many ways it presents a bigger problem than reality-based violence. There violence is presented as funny, and children don't see it as harmful. Moreover, in cartoons punishment for violence is rare and generally has no lasting bad effects. Consequently, violence in cartoons is one of the most imitated behaviors.[30] Additionally, children who watch lots of violence grow up to be inclined to violent behavior as adults. Prior to the 1970s, the problem was associated with male viewers much more than female viewers. However, in the 1970s, programs like *Charlie's Angels* and *Wonder Woman* appeared, featuring aggressive women, and the girls who watched these shows have grown up to be aggressive adults, involved in "more confrontations, shoving matches, chokings and knife fights" than women who did not watch those shows.[31] Indeed, women who are heavy violence watchers are twice as likely to throw things at their spouses compared to other women, and more than four times as likely to have physically attacked other adults compared to other women.[32]

Violence in music also has an effect on behavior. A nationwide survey following the murders at Colorado's Columbine High School found that 66 percent of teens ages 13–17 believe that violence in music contributed to the shootings.[33]

Wrestling is another activity that gets imitated. A 1994 study of elementary school children described their imitation of WWF fights. They tackled their opponents, turned their legs in the wrong direction, strangled then kicked them in the face and poked them in the eyes. The principals of the schools reported that many WWF moves resulted in such things as concussions, broken bones and being knocked out, and required professional medical care.[34] In addition to the story about Lionel Tate killing his friend, a seven-year-old boy in Texas clotheslined his three-year-old brother and killed him. He said he'd seen the move in wrestling matches on television.[35] A counselor at a pregnancy crisis center told of two 12-year-old girls who reported that their boyfriends put dog collars and leashes on them, tied their hands and wrists to the bed, did whatever they wanted to do to them and then had sex. Both girls said the boys had seen this on WWF wrestling.[36]

How about the slasher movies? Do they have any effect on viewers? While imitation of this grotesque violence is rare, there have been nine murders specifically described as copycat *Scream* killings.[37]

In addition to violent behavior, kids who watch violence treat their classmates rudely, threaten them and spread nasty rumors. Their teachers and peers describe them as the meanest kids.[38] The coarse language on TV is also imitated. Elementary school teachers tell me that kids routinely call each other "bitch," "slut" and "bastard."

Desensitization

Long-term doses of media violence create people who become immune to the reality of violence and who regard violence as an acceptable way to solve problems. This "desensitization" means that viewers are less disturbed by real-life violence and aggression, compared to people who do not watch media violence. Combining violence with pleasure worsens the condition. Slasher films, for example, combine the pleasurable scenes of sexual behavior with those of killing and gore, and viewers become immune to the ghastliness of the violence. In one study, a group of college men watched five films over a five-day period that showed violence against women. Another group did not watch the films. On the sixth day, all of the men watched a brutal documentary about a rape. Then, they filled out a questionnaire asking such things as:

Was this film degrading to women?

How much violence was in this film?

Was the victim of the rape valuable or worthless?

The men who watched the films judged the women to be less valuable compared to the men who had not seen the films. They also judged the film as less degrading to women compared to the men who had not seen the films.[39]

Dave Grossman, author of *Stop Teaching Our Kids to Kill* (Crown, 1999), commented: "We have raised a generation of barbarians who have learnt to associate violence with pleasure. All the time in movie theatres, when there is bloody violence, the young people laugh and cheer and keep right on eating popcorn and drinking soda."[40] Desensitization also means that viewers regard violence as an acceptable, not distressing, way to handle disputes.

Watching wrestling, for example, correlates with date fighting. For both male and female viewers, wrestling is associated with both starting and being a victim of a date fight, carrying a gun, alcohol use and fighting at school.[41]

Fear

In addition to imitation and desensitization, heavy viewers of violence come to believe that the world is a much more violent world than it really is. Some viewers suffer from nightmares and depression from the content of the media.[42] Take, for an example, the commercial I described earlier in which the heads of kids who were doing magic on stage exploded. This unmotivated kind of violence may be very scary to kids, especially very young kids. Imagine worrying that for no good reason your head might explode! Older kids, and even college students, report long term fear effects from watching scary movies such as slasher films or thrillers like *Jaws* or *Psycho*.[43]

Further, think of all the families that eat supper while watching the news on TV. Does this violence register with kids? Apparently, it does. In 1994, in a study of parents, 37 percent of them said that something the kids saw on the news frightened them. Many of them commented that their children had been upset by coverage of the war in the Persian Gulf. In the study, violence between strangers, including shootings, kidnappings and sexual assault, created the most fear. Violence in foreign lands, including war and famine, and natural disasters also frightened children. Tornadoes, earthquakes, floods and fires scared 25 percent of the children.[44] As a result, I would suspect that kids were frightened by the news following the bombing of the Federal Building in Oklahoma City in 1995. And the non-stop coverage of the terrorist attacks on the World Trade Center towers in 2001 must have scared many more children. Moreover, since the 1994 study, we have many more 24-hour-a-day news sources plus the ability to report news occurring as it happens. If the survey were repeated, the results might reveal even more fear. Interestingly, the older the children were, the more likely they were to be frightened by the news. Apparently, as kids mature, they realize that these things could actually happen to them.

—What You Can Do—

- Watch TV with your children and talk about violent images and language. Discuss with your children whether or not the violence was punished. Ask your children to tell you what would likely happen if the incident occurred in real life. Would the perpetrator be in jail? Would the victim be in pain or die?

- Discuss ways a character could have handled the dispute without violence.

- Carefully monitor cartoon violence. Discuss the differences between fantasy and reality with your children. Ask them whether these events could happen in real life.

- Don't assume that all Disney movies or "G" rated movies are "safe." Take the time to preview videos before your children watch them.

- Watch the commercials with your children. Chuck, a father of sons ages six and eight, told me that he mutes the commercials so his boys aren't affected by them. What he didn't realize is that the visual images are often more powerful than the words. Given that nearly one-third of the commercials that have children in them include some type of aggression, be there to talk to them about it.

- Find out which stores sell CDs that have been edited and restrict your children to buying at those stores.

- Read the lyrics before allowing your children to play the music.

- If your children are watching professional wrestling, explain the various special effects that are used in television production.

- Before taking your children to a movie, check out websites that review movies. "Kids-In-Mind," for example, independently rates movies on ten-point scales for sex and nudity, violence and gore, and profanity.

- If your children watch the news, explain to them that the news is a "show" to earn money, and that the news business thinks that reporting crime, disasters and murders will acquire viewers. Don't assume that if your children are young they don't know what the news is about or that they aren't paying attention to it.

- Talk with your children about what they see on the news. If they are upset, let them talk to you about it. Kids, ages six to ten, often get scared or depressed after watching the news.

- Use the V-chip that is now standard on TV screens 13 inches or larger. If your television isn't equipped with a V-chip, investigate a device such as the Weemote 2 that gives you control of the channels your children can access.

- Use a device such as TV Guardian that filters out profanity.

- Keep TV sets out of kids' bedrooms.

Chapter 4

Friends — Cute Anorexic Chicks *:

Health Issues and the Media

Prior to the introduction of Western television in 1995, women in Fiji valued strong, tall and sturdy bodies—bodies that worked hard. They regarded thinness as a sign of neglect. After Western television came to Fiji, things changed. By 1998, eating disorders afflicted 29 percent of the girls.[1] Prior to 1995, the incidence of bulimia, self-induced vomiting, was zero. By 1998, more than 11 percent of Fijan girls admitted to bulimia and 69 percent said they had dieted to lose weight.[2]

More than 80 percent of the Fijan girls said that watching TV affected how they felt about their bodies.[3] Eating disorders are just one of several health problems created by the media.

Anorexia and Bulimia

American women have not always obsessed over thinness. The "Gibson Girl" of the early 1900s measured 38-27-45, "fat" by today's standards.

*Billboard sign in Sioux Falls, South Dakota, 2001.

During the Depression and World War II, Americans favored stronger, more substantial bodies. After the war, Christian Dior came out with the thin "New Look," which required tight girdles and waist cinchers. Women wanted to look like the waif-like Audrey Hepburn. To be that thin, the daily diet of one teen supermodel of the time consisted of a head of lettuce, a pound of seedless grapes and three green peppers. The super-thin models frequently offer dieting advice in magazines, so messages about the importance of being thin assail readers.[4]

In addition, women on television, in films and other performers overwhelm viewers. Some of those women actually have suffered from eating disorders. One of the most well-known was Karen Carpenter of the singing duo, The Carpenters. In the 1970s and 1980s, she dazzled listeners with her music. The Carpenters won three Grammy Awards and made eight Gold Albums, five Platinum Albums and ten Gold Singles. In 1983, Karen died of complications from anorexia nervosa, the compulsion to lose weight by eating next to nothing. Karen's troubles started in 1967 when she went on a water diet. She dropped from 140 to 120 pounds on her 5-foot 4-inch frame. When people told her she looked great, she determined to lose more weight. In the fall of 1975, Karen weighed just 80 pounds, had to lie down between shows and collapsed on stage during a show in Las Vegas. Her wasted appearance shocked her audiences. In spite of her attempts to treat the disorder, she died in 1983 of cardiac arrest related to her anorexia.[5] Karen's death created unprecedented concern about and interest in the disorder.

Although the producers of TV's *Ally McBeal* denied that Calista Flockhart was anorexic, she was so thin and weak that she collapsed during the filming of the show. Former cast member, Courtney Thorne-Smith left the show because of the excessive dieting and exercising she was doing to be as thin as the other cast members. She feared that she was damaging her body.[6]

At age 19, Tracey Gold, who played Carol Seaver on *Growing Pains,* gained 15 pounds, not unusual for kids leaving home for the first time. The writers included her weight gain into scripts, writing "fat" jokes about her. The jokes upset the five-foot three-inch, 133-pound actress so much that she lost 20 pounds in two months. She continued dieting and by the last season of the show weighed only 80 pounds. She had to leave the program to be hospitalized for treatment.[7]

Jamie-Lynn Sigler, a daughter in HBO's *The Sopranos,* suffered from "exercise bulimia." She weighed a normal amount when the pilot was shot, but by the beginning of the first season she had lost a great deal of weight with her regimen of six to seven hours of daily exercise. Her health habits upset fellow cast members, and the show's creator even called her mother to ask if she were eating. She was so emaciated he feared he might have to replace her.[8]

Media images of extremely thin women powerfully affect readers and viewers. Magazine readers often fail to realize that the women in some photos are not only anorexic, they also have breast implants. In addition, the photos have been airbrushed or altered with computer software, so these images are simply not attainable by "real" women.[9] Unfortunately, constant exposure to these pictures makes women dissatisfied with their bodies. This dissatisfaction affects even very young readers. Ten-year-old girls say they are ashamed of their bodies.[10]

Girls and teens become preoccupied with their bodies, and they diet and develop eating disorders. In 1990, the average age a girl started dieting was eight, down from age 14 in 1970. Eighty-one percent of 10-year-old girls worry about getting fat.[11] Anorexia is difficult to cure. Even with treatment, 10 percent of anorexics die from the disorder.[12]

Boys and teens also obsess about their bodies and compare themselves to the muscle-bound and lean males in the media. They want to look like Arnold Schwarzenegger,

Sylvester Stallone or Jean-Claude Van Damme. Boys talk about developing their "six-pack" abdominal muscles and looking "cut." Even boys' action figures are bulked up. Today's Batman would measure a 30-inch waist, a 57-inch chest and 27-inch biceps.[13] To build muscle and look more like the guys in the Calvin Klein ads, up to 11 percent of high school boys use anabolic steroids. Boys and teens also fixate about their weight. Self-conscious about their bodies, high school boys skip showers after gym classes so other boys won't see them naked. A specialist in treating eating disorders estimates that one million American males experience anorexia or bulimia.[14]

Obesity

After being prescribed steroids to treat her asthma, second grader Lauren Makowski's weight reached 100 pounds. She couldn't sit in a regular school desk or fit into the swings on the playground. In third grade, her doctor prescribed Ritalin to help her cope with her fidgeting; Lauren gained another 60 pounds. Miserable, she was teased at school and came home crying. Eating was her only comfort. Her weight finally reached 292 pounds. Alysia Lopez , another youngster suffering from obesity, is five years old and at 3-feet 6-inches, weighs 90 pounds and wears a size 16. She shops in the teen clothing department. Her cholesterol tops 200, 30 points more than is desirable. Even brief walks give her shortness of breath. She runs a high risk of developing Type II diabetes—also called adult onset diabetes because it is generally found only in adults.[15] Type II diabetes carries with it dangers of blindness, kidney failure, amputation, heart attacks and stroke. The disease afflicts approximately 300,000 children. Other health problems children face because of obesity include gallbladder disease, high cholesterol and sleep apnea.[16]

Pediatricians call childhood obesity an epidemic. Health professionals describe children as obese if they weigh 20 percent more than their ideal weight.[17] Ten percent of preschoolers weigh more than they should,[18] and obesity in kids five to eight years old rose from 10 percent in 1990 to 40 percent in 1997.[19] One expert concludes that because of the epidemic "for the first time in over a century, today's kids will not live as long as their parents." [20]

As one might expect, television, video games and the Internet contribute significantly to this epidemic. Two-to five-year-old children watch, on average, 25 hours of TV a week. This watching contributes to obesity in several ways. First, watching TV is not exercise and burns very few calories.[21] It also cuts into leisure time that would be better used doing sports or games. A recent Harvard study asked kids ages 11 to 13 to estimate how much time they spent in vigorous exercise during a day. The kids reported an average of one hour. However, when the researchers attached motion recorders to the kids they learned that the average was two minutes![22] The kids had vastly overestimated the time they spent exercising.

Second, commercials for high-fat, high-calorie and high-sugar items dominate the shows kids watch.[23] During kids' most popular viewing times, food commercials make up the majority of TV advertising. On Saturday mornings, one food commercial runs every five minutes, mostly for high-calorie items loaded with fat and sugar, such as McDonald's burgers and Frosted Flakes.[24]

Third, kids often snack while they watch TV, and compared to 20 years ago, snacks come in bigger packages, containing more calories.[25] Overweight children may have learned to associate eating with watching TV from infancy when busy mothers propped their bottles while the children were in front of a TV set. Indeed, many kids watch TV while eating meals. Black children eat 62 percent of their meals while watching TV. This compares to Latino children (43 percent), White children (32 percent) and Asian American children (21 percent). Watching television while eating contributes to obesity because watchers fail to realize when they are full. Children of normal weight eat half as many dinners in front of the TV compared to overweight children.[26]

In response to this obesity epidemic, retailers have created plus-size clothes for children. In 2001, sales of plus-size clothes for kids amounted to $2.5 billion and accounted for close to 10 percent of the kids clothing market. These lines of clothing appear in trendy stores like The Limited and The Gap, as well as Sears and Wal-Mart. Plus sizes accounted for 10 percent of The Limited's total sales.[27]

Cosmetic Surgery

Will Britney Spears, Jennifer Aniston, Christina Aguilera and J. Lo still be the rage in 10 years? Perhaps not. But a lot of young women who look like them will remind us of their popularity. Although relatively uncommon, plastic surgery for teens increased from 2.9 percent of the plastic surgeries in 1997 to 3.5 percent in 2000. Although that is less than a 1 percent rise, it's actually a 20 percent increase.[28]

Plastic surgeons observe that teens ask to look like popular media stars. In 2003, they want a round butt like J. Lo and Jennifer Aniston's operated-on nose. Not too long ago, everyone wanted to look like Sharon Stone.[29] In 2002, the most sought-after jawline and chin belonged to Cate Blanchett. Women wanted Heather Locklear's nose and Britney Spears' whole body.[30] Pamela Anderson of *Baywatch* fame made breast augmentation popular.[31] A California plastic surgeon says many of his patients use the looks of celebrities to guide their makeovers. The irony is that almost all of the celebrities have had plastic surgery.[32]

Sommer Seidel wanted to look more like her teen media idols, which for her included having sizeable breasts. She waited until she finished high school to get the implants that increased her cup size from a "B" to a "C."[33] Ever since Jennifer Ebell took a TV class in high school, she's dreamed of being a broadcast journalist but feels that her puffy eyes don't conform to the industry standard. She thinks the puffiness makes her look sleepy, so she's having her eyelids surgically altered.[34] Even young teens alter their bodies. Maggie changed many of her physical attributes with plastic surgery. As an eighth grader, she got a nose job. At 17, liposuction improved her flabby chin and removed her buccal fat pads, the pads of fat just under the cheekbones. They keep a person from looking really gaunt as an adult, but Maggie had them removed. She had breast augmentation when she finished high school, and now she says she feels great.[35]

Girls aren't the only ones who seek out plastic surgery. In the quest for the muscular builds of male media idols, in addition to using anabolic steroids, boys want pec implants, plastic surgery on their noses and liposuction to remove baby fat.[36]

Nutrition and Alcohol Use

Children receive subtle messages about nutrition and alcohol use from the way television and film portray their use. I did a study of the nutritional messages embedded in *The Cosby Show*, *Family Ties* and *Growing Pains*, three popular and highly praised sitcoms during the 1986–1987 season. I wanted to find out what subtle messages about health kids get from these shows. I was surprised to find that, on the shows, the kids ate more nutritious food than the adults. The kids often ate apples or oranges or drank fruit juice after school. They ate cereal for breakfast and healthy brown bag lunches at school. On the other hand, the adults ate donuts and drank coffee for breakfast, skipped lunch and drank soft drinks. Unfortunately, the most frequently eaten meal by both kids and adults was the "snack," consisting of chips, crackers, popcorn and soft drinks. Viewers tend to imitate the behaviors they see on TV, so in this case, although kids ate healthier food than adults, the snacking is a problem, because heavy snacking is associated with obesity.[37]

During the 1998–1999 television season, 77 percent of the episodes of the most popular prime time shows included references to alcohol, and 51 percent of the major characters drank alcohol. These characters were more attractive and had higher status than characters who did not drink.[38] *Cheers* may be the best-known television show with many references to alcohol. Although no longer seen in first run, its 11 seasons of programs are widely available in syndication and on cable such as *Nick at Nite*. This program, set in a bar, features the heavily drinking characters of Norm, frequently unemployed; Cliff, a letter carrier; and Frasier, a psychiatrist. The characters spend hours in the Cheers bar drinking beer, which has no ill effects. Norm drinks the most, and his beer drinking is so excessive that in real life it would damage his body. However, we never see these bad effects. Indeed, a normal part of everyday life for the *Cheers* characters is to overindulge in beer. Viewers are encouraged to see this drinking as normal by the presence of the laugh track. It lets viewers see the drinking as comical.[39]

Television ads for alcohol portray drinking as a positive experience. Groups of very attractive young adults relax in bars and enjoy sporting events while drinking a beer. Most kids who see these ads conclude that alcohol creates positive experiences. A study of 10- and 11-year-olds published in 1994 concluded that the positive portrayal of alcohol use on television strongly affected kids' ideas about drinking and their intent to drink alcohol themselves.[40]

A study published in 1998 found nearly 80 percent of all films show at least one key character drinking alcohol. Moreover, in 93 percent of the movies rented in 1996 and 1997, characters drank alcohol. In more than half of those movies the alcohol use did not cause any problems such as car accidents or getting into fights.[41]

Another study examined all "G" rated animated films released between 1937 and 2000. The researchers learned that characters drank alcohol in nearly half of the movies including such classics as *Fantasia* (1940), *Pinocchio, Dumbo* and *Sleeping Beauty*. Characters also drank in more recent films such as *The Great Mouse Detective, All Dogs Go to Heaven* and *Beauty and the Beast*. The portrayal was often for humor, and no negative consequences occurred. Recent animated movies feature less alcohol use than earlier ones, but given that all of them are available for rental, its portrayal should concern parents.[42]

Although the depiction of alcohol use in films may not cause kids to drink, it's alarming that one in seven 4th graders has been drunk and that one in three believes that, among their peers, drinking is a considerable problem.[43]

Tobacco Use and Illicit Drugs

In recent years the use of tobacco on television has been rare, compared to the early days of television. In the 1950s and 1960s, major characters in television sitcoms, dramas and variety shows, routinely smoked. Desi Arnaz of *I Love Lucy*, Jack Webb of *Dragnet*, Milton Berle, Ed Sullivan and George Burns of variety show fame, all smoked on screen. During the 1980s, characters on TV smoked only once every three hours. In the 1990s more characters smoked, but the occurrence was still rare compared to the 1950s and 1960s. However, with cable outlets offering many reruns of the early shows, kids once again see a lot of smoking. Successful White males tend to be the smokers, offering desirable role models for kids.[44]

Smoking occurs much more frequently in films than on TV, and it appears glamorous. Humphrey Bogart in *Casablanca* made the act of smoking irresistibly sexy. More recently, smoking stars include the James Bond character in *License to Kill*, the Lois Lane character in *Superman II*, actress Jennifer Beal in *Flashdance,* actress Sharon Stone in *Basic Instinct*, actress Glenn Close in *Fatal Attraction* and actor Sylvester Stallone in three of his films.[45] A study of "G" rated animated films found that nearly half of them feature the use of tobacco. The popular *Pinocchio, Dumbo, Alice in Wonderland, One Hundred and One Dalmatians, The Great Mouse Detective* and *Little Nemo: Adventures in Slumberland,* all feature tobacco use.[46] Currently, smoking in the top-grossing movies exceeds the rate of portrayal in the 1960s. Before the Surgeon General's 1964 report on the dangers of smoking, tobacco use appeared once every five minutes. In the 1970s and 1980s, it appeared once every 10 to 15 minutes, and in the 1990s it increased to once every three to five minutes.[47]

There is good evidence that the smoking in movies impacts kids' smoking habits. One study followed 2,600 adolescents who had never smoked as of 1999, the start of the study. The researchers found that within two years, 107 of those who watched movies with a lot of smoking started to smoke, compared to just 22 of those who watched movies with very little smoking. The researchers concluded that watching movies that included smoking had a greater effect on kids' likelihood to smoke than even cigarette advertising and promotion.[48]

Although drug use is portrayed less often than smoking, a study of the top-rated television shows of the 1998–1999 season found that 20 percent of the shows mentioned or showed drugs, and 3 percent showed actual drug use. For example, *ER, That '70s Show* and *The Wayans Brothers* have shown marijuana use. Negative consequences of drug use occurred in only two-thirds of the shows.[49] A study of 200 top movie rentals in 1996 and 1997 found that about 20 percent of them, including *Trainspotters, Pulp Fiction, Tommy Boy* and *Face-Off*, showed illicit drug use. Fifteen percent of the movies showed drug use associated with luxury and wealth, and featured drug use in a positive light. In over half the instances, no negative consequences resulted from drug use.[50]

Hearing Loss

In remote parts of Africa, men in their 70s can hear sounds as soft as a whisper across the length of a football field.[51] That level of hearing acuity probably doesn't exist in America, because exposure to high levels of noise causes hearing loss in millions of Americans.

Inside the ear is a snail-shaped organ called the cochlea, and it is filled with fluid and lined with tiny cells. From each cell, a hair-like thread extends into the fluid. As sound waves from the environment hit the eardrum, they pass through the bones of the inner ear and enter the cochlea.[52] Different pitches of sound trigger vibrations in different hair cells, which communicate to the cells on the lining and send electrical signals to the brain. The brain perceives these electrical impulses as sound.

The system works fine if the volume (measured in decibels, dB) of the sound is in a safe range, but exposure to sounds over 85 decibels (e.g. a power mower) for more than a couple of minutes damages hearing. Loud sounds injure or destroy those tiny hair cells, and destroyed hair cells can't send messages to the cells that produce electrical signals in the brain. The hearing loss is most acute in the pitches we need to hear to have normal conversations.[53] I notice this deficiency in many of my students; and every year, when I use a DVD in class, I must increase the volume more than I did the year before. Hearing loss is not only permanent and untreatable, it's also cumulative. This means that exposure to several rock concerts does not make a person "immune" to the damage. Because the earlier rock concerts caused hearing loss, the new rock concert no longer sounds really loud. However, the ear still processes all of those decibels and more damage occurs.

Loud sounds also cause tinnitus, a constant ringing in the ears. It also can't be treated. Every semester several of my students describe their lives with it. It never goes away and distresses them most when they study or try to sleep.

The use of headsets to drown out other noise, such as that of airplanes or the subway, provides one of the greatest hazards to hearing. At full volume, personal stereos hit nearly 140 dBs, much louder than the 85 dBs that damage hearing. Other dangerous sources of noise include computer games (up to 135 dB), video arcades (up to 110 dB) and loud action movies (usually above 90dB). Additionally, many kids' toys produce damaging noise. Squeak toys can hit up to 110dB, musical toys measure 120 dB, and some toy phones ring at nearly 130 dB.[54] Also, cars with excessive stereo systems easily reach 130 dB.[55] Some music in the cars adolescents drive is so loud that at a stop sign the cars vibrate. Even with all of the windows closed, the music can easily be heard by people in the next car.

Musicians especially risk hearing loss. Rockers Pete Townsend, John Lee Hooker and members of Metallica and Aerosmith all suffer from permanent hearing loss. The avante-garde group Mission of Burma disbanded after the guitarist, Roger Miller, developed tinnitus.[56] Hearing loss forced Phil Collins, the former Genesis drummer, to quit touring. He rarely performs live in an effort to preserve what hearing he does have. Also, former president Bill Clinton blames his hearing loss on playing in bands and going to rock concerts.[57] Kathy Peck, a singer with The Contractions, a band that opened for Duran Duran, developed ringing in her ears that lasted for days. She finally couldn't hear at all. Ten years later, laser surgery restored some of her hearing. Since then, she has co-founded Hearing Education and Awareness for Rockers (H.E.A.R.) to get the word out about the connection between music and deafness.[58]

Classical musicians risk hearing loss as well. A 1991 study found that more than 50 percent of the musicians in the Chicago Symphony Orchestra suffered from major hearing loss. In fact, their rigorous rehearsal and performance schedules put them at greater risk than rockers. High school band players also acquire hearing loss, and some dedicated musicians suffer permanent hearing loss as young as age 10.[59]

While television isn't as big a hearing risk as personal stereos and rock concerts, damage to ones hearing occurs when a TV is turned up so that it can be heard over some other noise-producing devices such as vacuum cleaners, dishwashers or washing machines.

Ergonomics

When seven-year-old Carl plays computer games, he uses his mom's computer. He perches himself on the edge of her computer chair, dangles his legs and feet above the floor, and cranes his neck to look at the monitor.

Experts in ergonomics, the study of the relationship between a person's body and his/her workplace, find that computer use and playing computer games create physical problems for kids. A study of 95 third–fifth grade students found that none of them used computer work stations properly for postural comfort. Kids develop neck and back aches from using keyboards and monitors that are placed too high.[60] Using an adult's computer chair means a kid has no back support, which causes postural problems. If the chair has arm rests, they will be too high for a child.[61] Also, eye doctors find that computer use impedes kids' visual development.[62] Kids risk developing carpal tunnel syndrome, and many kids already suffer from pain at the base of their thumbs from playing computer games.[63] Excessive computer game play also stresses the knuckles at the base of the fingers and causes tendonitis in the thumbs.[64]

—What You Can Do—

- Discuss the problem of media's obsession with thinness with your children. Be critical of those unhealthy images.

- Explain how photos of ultra-thin models are often air-brushed or altered by a computer to make the women appear so thin, and reveal the fact that many models have breast implants.

- Eat dinner at home, as a family, at a table, without television.

- Limit TV viewing to one to two hours of television daily, and you will limit your child's exposure to many ads for unhealthy foods.

- If your child is influenced by the looks of a media idol and wants plastic surgery, learn about the risks as well as benefits and discuss them with your child.

- Point out to your children how unlikely it is for TV characters to eat all the time and still be thin. Be critical of the food choices TV characters make and of how much snacking occurs.

- Discuss the unrealistic portrayal of drinking alcohol, smoking tobacco and using illicit drugs. Talk to your children about the real-life consequences of their use.

- Explain that movie stars are frequently paid by tobacco companies to smoke on-screen.

- Use the websites that review movies, including www.moviemom.com, www.screenit.com and others to determine if a movie is appropriate for your children.

- If your children have personal stereos, make sure the machines include high quality headphones that block out the environmental noise. This will lessen the need to crank the volume of the music to dangerous levels.

- Insist that your children use ear protection at rock concerts. Cotton balls and wadded up tissues do nothing to protect ears. Also, if your child is a musician, invest in the special musicians' earplugs. They range from $30–$150 per pair, far cheaper than the several thousand dollars cost of hearing aids.

- Modify your computer workstation for your children's use. This may include taking your monitor off the monitor stand and placing it directly on the desk top. Your children's eyes should be level with the monitor. Make the computer chair fit them better by putting pillows under their bottoms and behind their backs. Invest in a keyboard that is scaled down in size for your children's hands. Child-sized mouses are also available, and some experts recommend that you teach your children to use the mouse with their non-dominant hand.

- Check your children's posture as they use computers. They should have straight backs; their feet should be flat on the floor or footrest; and their knuckles, wrists and the tops of their forearms should be in a straight line.

- Use an anti-glare screen so your children don't develop vision problems such as squinting and eyestrain.

- Keep your children a safe distance from the computer screen—two to four feet away is recommended.

Chapter 5

Has Anything Changed Since *Charlie's Angels,*
Amos 'n' Andy or *Chico and the Man?*

Media Stereotypes

When Jeff Valdez, presently the producer of Nickelodeon's *The Brothers Garcia*, and other Latino themed programs, was a kid in a Denver housing project, the appearance of a Latino character on television was so rare that his mom called him in from outdoor play to watch. He and his friends would run into the house to look, marveling at this wonderful affirmation of their self-worth. Sadly, diversity is still rare on prime time television.[1] Furthermore, stereotypical portrayals of many groups are common.

Portrayal of Gender

The Portrayal of Women

Betty Friedan's 1963 book, *The Feminine Mystique* (Dell, 1964), contributed greatly to the women's liberation movement. As support for the movement grew, women made demands, not only for workplace and political power, but also for changes in the media's portrayal of women. Until that point, the media had depicted women as helpless, beautiful, thin, young and dumb.[2] *The Mary Tyler Moore Show* (1970–1977) made moves toward workplace power. In one episode, Mary complained to her boss, Lou Grant, that he paid her less than he paid her predecessor. Her boss argued that her predecessor (a male) had a family to support. She almost bought the argument, but then countered that the pay of bachelors was equal to that of married men, so her treatment was unfair. For the 1970s, a successful argument for equal pay was a major victory.[3] Another '70s show featuring a strong woman was *Maude* (1972–1978). Strong, bright and politically progressive, *Maude* addressed thorny issues such as menopause and abortion. In one episode, she had the chance to run for the Senate and her husband objected. She chose the Senate race over her husband, and as a result, he left her. Much of the show focused on her conflicted life torn between the traditional role of women and her own career goals.[4]

Despite the progress made by *Mary Tyler Moore* and *Maude*, the feminist movement got sidetracked by the sexual revolution, represented on shows heavy into the "jiggle factor" or tits and ass (T and A) shows. *Three's Company* was one such show. Between 1977 and 1984 *Three's Company* featured two sexy women, Janet Wood and Chrissy Snow, and a man, Jack Tripper, as roommates. The women's parents and the landlords opposed this setup, so, to alleviate the opposition, the man posed as a homosexual, not attracted to the women. The program relied on sexual innuendo, misunderstandings and sexist plots for its popularity. It is still seen on Nick at Night.[5] Another tits and ass show was *Charlie's Angels* (1976–1981). Although the show tried to position itself as featuring strong women, the feminist values were undermined by braless and seductive women. Farrah Fawcett's nipples were featured prominently, and the three women relied on sex appeal, seduction and sexist stereotypes to go undercover and solve crimes. Charlie, the millionaire for whom the angels worked, talked in sexual innuendos and gave the angels instructions while sipping cocktails served to him by scantily clad women.[6]

In the 1980s, *Cagney and Lacey* (1982–1988) portrayed the rare professional women on television.[7] The show featured two three-dimensional female characters and tackled serious issues. For instance, several episodes explored the challenges Lacey faced in balancing work and family, the stresses she faced as her children matured and the difficulties of the two women finding a place in the predominantly male world of cops.[8] In contrast, while *The Golden Girls* (1985–1992) featured four women aged 50 and older, the plots mostly revolved around finding men. For example, the doctor who treated Sophia's high blood pressure enchanted both Dorothy and Blanche. Blanche planned her wedding to Harry, only to learn that he was a bigamist. And Rose worried about sharing a stateroom with Arnie on a cruise to the Bahamas.[9] These characters focused on romance and the importance of having men in their lives. *Murphy Brown* (1988–1998) featured a tough, competent, aggressive female reporter who got into jams, not because she was some dumb blonde, but because of her personality as Murphy.[10]

In spite of the professional feminist character of Murphy, *Baywatch* (1989–1996) marked another step backward for feminism. This program featured sexy men and women lifeguards in red swim suits. The women's chests bulged out of their suits, most notably Pamela Anderson's breasts, which were augmented with implants. One critic maintained that Anderson's presence on television insulted women and represented a decline of Western civilization. In spite of the criticism, *Baywatch* is the most-watched television show ever. It is still on in syndication—worldwide it claims a billion viewers.[11]

When it comes to entertainment specifically for kids, most parents assume that Disney movies are safe fare for their children. However, close examination of recent Disney movies find them to be acutely sexist. *The Little Mermaid*

(1989), one of many Disney girls without mothers, must find
a man in order to be fulfilled. In this movie, Ursula the witch
tells Ariel that men don't listen to women so it would be a
good deal to sacrifice her voice to get her man. In addition,
Ursula persuades Ariel to abandon her family and alter her
body to get a man.[12] In *Aladdin* (1992), Aladdin regards
Jasmine as an object of desire and thinks that marrying her
will help his position in society. He does, and in addition to
improving Aladdin's position, the marriage to Aladdin as-
sures her happiness. In *The Lion King* (1994), male characters rule the kingdom and female characters do their bid-
ding. *Pocahontas* (1995) appears as a curvaceous woman
and, not as John Smith's captive, but rather as a participant
in a love affair with him. In another captive scenario, the
Beast in *Beauty and the Beast* (1991), captures Belle, who
then tames him and falls in love with him.[13]

More recently, a 2002 television report indicates that
male characters outnumber female characters, and twice as
many programs feature the male point of view compared to
the female point of view. Male characters run the government, police departments, schools, department stores—essentially, males run the world. Furthermore, while some
shows, such as *Judging Amy* (1999–2005) and *The West Wing*
(1999–2006) feature strong female characters, the gap between those positive characterizations and the bottom of the
pit has widened.[14] On *The Bachelor* (2002–present), one man
is presented with 25 attractive women who say they can't
find a man on their own and are willing to settle for a total
stranger. They participate in a "marital meat market" in
which the bachelor spends a little time with the group of
women. Then the bachelor chooses 15 of the 25 to remain
in the competition. In the series of episodes featuring "Alex,"
viewers saw Alex making out with and lying on top of woman
after woman. After six weeks of "tryouts" of the 15 women,
Alex chose one to actually marry.

WWF Smackdown (1999–present) has featured Val Venis,

whose nickname for his penis is "Big Valbowski." On one show he encouraged the women in the audience to donate to the Big Valbowski mutual fund—it's always up. A wrestler called X-Pac wore a shirt that read, "Suck It," and he pointed to his crotch. Another one dressed as a pimp and brought a following of "Ho Train" women dressed as whores in sleazy clothes. Female wrestlers wear extremely seductive clothing—pants falling off their hips, revealing tiny G-strings and a female called The Cat (read "pussy") nearly stripped on stage. Female wrestlers also brawl in Bra and Panty matches, in which the wrestlers strip their opponents to their underwear to win the match. In addition, the recent *Survivor: The Amazon* (2002) reality program pitted the men against the women, resulting in base stereotypical behavior by both groups. The women removed their bikini tops in order to bathe in full view of the men. In another scene, three women declared that if they needed to show some skin to win the game that would be no problem. They figured if they strutted their boobs and tight bodies, the men would be less likely to vote them off the show. The men engaged in locker room chat about which girls were "hottest" and who they'd like to hook up with.[15]

Critics have also attacked the very popular program, *Ally McBeal,* (1997–2002) as "the most regressive female presence on television since Edith Bunker." They noted that in spite of her career as an attorney, Ally's overpowering aim is to find a man, and the women on the show are bitchy catfighters.[16] A bevy of men parade through the lives of the women on *Friends* (1994–2004). Although Rachel had a long-term relationship with Ross, she had 12 other boyfriends during the series. Monica, who married Chandler, had 10 other boyfriends, and Phoebe had 12 boyfriends. A weblog for "Elaine's Boyfriends" on *Seinfeld* (1989–98) describes 27 of them.

Buffy, the Vampire Slayer (1997–2003), now in syndication, features Buffy and her friends who every week save the citizens of their town, Sunnnydale, CA. Screenwriter Joss Whedon claims he purposely created a strong feminist character who could serve as a model for kids. He wanted a twist on the typical horror genre in which the dumb girl gets accosted in a dark alley. Instead he made a girl who could go into the dark alley and beat the evil-doers. Many critics have praised *Buffy*, as well as *Xena: Warrior Princess* (1995–2001) for its empowerment of females. Others object to Buffy's skill at martial arts because it simply confirms the values of men and maleness.[17] Still others reject Buffy as a feminist because she wears skimpy costumes that display her cleavage and describe her as a "girlie girl through and through."[18]

The contradictory reactions to "Buffy" reflect the differences between what has come to be called Third Wave feminism compared to Second Wave feminism. Historically, First Wave feminists were those who sought the vote. Second Wave feminists fought for equal pay for equal work, better child care options and representation in politics. Third Wave feminists (the daughters of the Second Wave feminists) take for granted equal rights and equal pay and assert that women should be relishing their sexuality. They embrace Buffy as an example of a feminist who values her sexuality. These feminists appreciate the sex kittens and those who aspire to be like Madonna.[19] They call themselves "Do-Me's" and "lipstick feminists." In addition to praise for Buffy, Third Wave feminists applaud *The Powerpuff Girls* (1998–present). They claim that the three five-year-old girls exemplify strong women who can "kick ass and take names" and still retain their femininity.[20] On the other hand, critics note that each of the characters exemplifies a typical sexist gender stereotype. They assert that one is girlishly sweet, another is the tomboy and the third is stereotypically "girl" smart.[21] So viewers of the media respond very differently to television women, depending on their connection with Second or Third Wave feminists.

In addition to sexist portrayals and the emphasis on finding a man, female characters on TV are younger than male characters, sending a message to women that their value rests largely in appearance and youth. Female characters do appear in a greater variety of careers than on earlier TV shows,[22] but they still turn up mostly in the traditional roles of maid, teacher or secretary. Furthermore, a study of the 2001–2002 season found that there were only four females in science or technology professions during the hours in prime time that children tend to watch.[23] An earlier study of all of prime time dramatic television aired during the 1994–1997 seasons found that White men played 75 percent of all scientists, compared to just 13 percent of White women.[24] Given the influence television has on children's expectations about the real world, one can anticipate that few girls aspire to be scientists.

The Portrayal of Men

Although men appear on television more often than women, they aren't always seen in positive roles. A 1999 report found that kids ages 10 to 17 described the males on television as violent and angry. The older brother on *Malcolm in the Middle* (2000–2006) was sent to military school because he caused so much trouble. Although *South Park* (1997–present) includes a warning that this is an adult program, teens and kids love the show. At the end of every episode for most of the seasons, the character Kenny got killed off in various ways—hit by a bus, crushed by a falling piano and shot by a SWAT team, for example.

Analysis of the male characters on TV done by Children NOW, also found them to be leaders, problem solvers, confident, successful and athletic. These characteristics appear on television, in movies, in music videos and in video games. The rigidity of these characteristics creates a tough act for boys to follow as they grow to manhood. Television also portrays males as obsessed with sex. If a guy doesn't get laid, he's a loser.[25] For instance, *Friends* features male characters fixated on sex, and both male and female characters engage in casual sex.

Another common male image on TV is that of the bumbling adult male. Homer, on *The Simpsons* (1989–present), always messes up his work at the power plant or looks to Marge to bail him out of jams. Raymond, on *Everybody Loves Raymond* (1996–present), is dominated by his wife Debra and his overbearing mother, who lives right across the street from them. *Malcolm in the Middle* also features an incompetent dad in a family dominated by the mother. Both of these shows focus on men trying to appease women.

Disney movies also provide problematic images of males. Virtually all Disney films favor masculine versions of power. For instance, all of the rulers of the kingdom in *The Lion King* are males who subordinate women. The male characters lead, and the female characters just follow the wishes of the males.[26]

Portrayals of Racial and Ethnic Minorities

Although people of color currently make up over 30 percent of the U.S. population, they are rarely seen on television.[27] Children learn whether or not their race is valued by observing whether characters of color are shown on TV. Kids learn about their racial identity's importance by how often they see characters of color and whether the portrayals are positive or negative.[28] Furthermore, White kids learn about people of color from television as well. A study of over 300 White children found that 60 percent of them thought that TV's portrayal of Black people was accurate—that Black people talk and act like those on TV.[29]

The Portrayal of Blacks

The Cosby Show (1984–1991) featured two successful professional people and their children, and both Black and White audiences enjoyed the program. But after it left the air, the decade of the '90s was a decade of mediocrity for Blacks on prime time television. On *Fresh Prince of Bel-Air* (1990–1996), the Black character Carlton was the butt of many jokes because he lacked street smarts and used big words. Blacks were featured in simple-minded and offensive comedies like *Martin* (1992–1997). Martin was an anti-feminist like Archie Bunker who talked ghetto talk and was dumb.[30] Viewers criticized *The PJs* (1999–2001) that featured a poor Black family living in the projects as degrading and humiliating to Blacks. Spike Lee called it "hateful" toward Blacks. Some critics called it a reincarnation of *Amos 'n' Andy* (1951–1953) and equally as offensive, based on the premise that poor Black people are somehow innately comic.[31]

A study of the 1999 TV season concluded that Black characters appeared in sitcoms but very rarely were in dramas. Furthermore, the cable networks UPN and WB accounted for 44 percent of the Black characters on TV.[32] Then, in 2000, the NAACP examined the 26 new series in the prime time TV lineup and found that none of them had minorities in leading roles or were aimed at a minority audience. Kweisi Mfume, the head of the NAACP, attacked the networks for this omission and successfully forced them to agree to promote more racial diversity on television.[33] The protest brought positive results, and the 2001–2002 television season featured many Black characters in both leading and supporting roles. They play attorneys, physicians and a military commander, for example, on both network and cable outlets.[34]

Many Disney movies are also racially insensitive. In *The Lion King,* the talk of the hyenas sounds like gang speech.[35] The members of the royal family speak in snooty British accents, whereas the hyenas feature the voices of Whoopi Goldberg and Cheech Marin using the accents of street talk. Disney has traditionally created offensive portrayals of Blacks, dating back to the 1946 *Song of the South* and the 1967 *The Jungle Book.*[36]

The Portrayal of Latinos

Although the Latino population in America is now the largest minority group in the country, Latinos accounted for only 4 percent of the regular characters on prime time TV in the 2002–2003 season. Since *Chico and the Man* (1974–1978) left the air, Latinos have been rare on prime time TV. While in the fall 2002 line-up two shows featuring Latino characters, *The George Lopez Show* and *Greetings from Tucson,* represented just 2 percent of the prime time series, these two shows included 44 percent of all Latino characters on prime time. The cancellation of *Tucson* dramatically reduced the number of Latino characters.[37] A study of the 2003–2004 season found that only 3 percent of the prime time characters on the four major networks were Latino.[38] Furthermore, when Latino characters do appear, they often take negative roles such as gangsters, drug dealers, sexy women and maids, and they usually have stereotypical Hispanic accents.

One of the few positive occupations of Latinos is as a government agent. Jimmy Smits, for example, played a detective for many years on *N.Y.P.D. Blue.* In addition, they are over-represented in the service worker, unskilled worker and criminal categories.[39] Lopez notes that no person of color is a regular on *Friends,* although it takes place in New York City, a city heavily populated with people of color. He also notes the contradiction in having no Cubans on *CSI: Miami* (2002–present), a city with many Cubans.[40]

The Portrayal of Native Americans

Debbie Reese, a Pueblo Indian who grew up in the northern part of New Mexico, lived and went to school with other Native Americans, as well as Latino and White children. When she was a doctoral student at the University of Illinois, an area with few Native Americans, her daughter was in preschool. She recalled picking up her daughter from school one day, only to find the little girl outraged by the illustration in a George and Martha book of what she called a "TV Indian." As time passed, Debbie learned that most young kids believe either that all the Native Americans are dead or that they actually wear Indian headdresses, and ride horses rather than drive cars. Children who don't grow up with any Native Americans believe these stereotypes, and they get these ideas from television, books and other media that display these images.[41]

The 2000 census revealed that although 1 percent of the U.S. population was Native American, during the 2001–2002 prime time television season, only 0.3 percent of the primary characters were Native American.[42] A report by the group, American Indians in Film & Television, found that in the 2003–2004 season virtually no Native Americans were portrayed on TV and in the movies.[43] In the early days of television, western series such as *Gunsmoke* (1955–1975), *Wagon Train* (1957–1965) and *Cheyenne* (1955–1962) portrayed Native Americans as savages and killers. The best known Native American was undoubtedly Tonto, the sidekick of *The Lone Ranger* (1949–1957), who had very limited language skills. Much later, *Dr. Quinn, Medicine Woman* (1993–1998), included a Native American named Cloud Dancing, played by a Native American who said that the producers wanted him to speak stereotypical "pidgin English," but he refused. Perhaps the least stereotypical portrayals were the characters Marilyn Whirlwind and Ed Chigliak on *Northern Exposure* (1990–1995). However, critics observed that the show stole bits and pieces of many native cultures and, although set in Alaska, did not accurately portray the Native Alaskan culture.[44]

Disney movies also portray Native Americans in negative stereotypical ways. *Pocahontas* (1995) lacks physical features that would identify her as a Native American. *Pochahontas* even includes a tune that contains a line, "Savages, savages!/Barely even human!"[45] A review of the recent video release of *Peter Pan* (1953) notes the negative stereotypical portrayal of the Native Americans as "crude caricatures" and includes a tasteless song called, "What Makes a Red Man Red."[46]

During the 2001–2002 season, only seven of over 3,000 prime time characters were Native Americans, and when they did appear they were cast as spiritual advisors. In real life, they hold jobs as doctors, teachers, cab drivers and lawyers, but as Native American actor Sonny Skyhawk noted, "we are always being portrayed as savages in loincloths." Native American children, watching television, claim that they receive messages that they shouldn't be seen, or that they are poor, drunk, living on reservations, dancing around fires and driving pickup trucks.[47]

The Portrayal of Asians

In the summer of 2003, FOX TV Stations began airing *Banzai*, which parodies Japanese game shows and blatantly stereotypes Asians. The narrator uses an outrageous Asian accent, and the participants are Asians who make hideous faces and strike martial arts poses.[48] In response to critical messages from viewers, Fox gagged all negative messages to the Fox Message Board. (Gagging refers to the practice of allowing messages to be seen by the sender of the message, but by no one else reading the board.) One viewer contacted an official at Sony, one of the show's sponsors, and urged her to watch the show. The official was so offended she pulled Sony's sponsorship.[49] It no longer airs. The Media Action Network for Asian Americans (MANAA) described a number of negative Asian stereotypes on TV and in films.

Asian characters typically aren't acculturated to American life and speak with heavy accents. Furthermore, while in real life Asian Americans enjoy a variety of professions, in the media they are in lower class jobs such as laundry workers, grocers and cab drivers. Think of Apu Nahasapeemapetilon, the Pakistani convenience store worker on *The Simpsons*. The racial features and accents of Asian characters are typically portrayed as comic or evil. In the Fu Manchu movies of the 1960s, the Asian characters appeared as inherently evil. In addition, TV and film portray Asian men as asexual, while the women are often the love interest for White men. The media show Asian women as exotic and subservient—often as a "China doll" or a geisha girl. In addition, programs such as *Chicago Hope* (1994–2000), *L.A. Law* (1986–1994) and *Murphy Brown*, set in large cities like Chicago or New York, are devoid of Asian characters.[50] On the opposite end of the spectrum, they may be shown as over-achievers. During the 2001–2002 season, most Asian/Pacific Islanders were shown as physicians, attorneys, nurses and small business owners.[51]

Although it took 60 years for Disney to produce an animated film featuring Asians, the movie *Mulan* was generally praised for featuring Mulan as a strong female who revered her father. When he was crippled in battle, she dressed as a boy and took his place in battle to save his life.

The Portrayal of Middle Easterners

Following the terrorist attacks of September 11, 2001, the portrayal of Arab and Muslim characters in the media became horrible. President George W. Bush actually asked FOX New Channel to feature stories about hunting down terrorists on two episodes of *America's Most Wanted* (1998–present). As a result, those two shows accounted for almost 40 percent of the Middle Easterners' portrayals on prime time during the 2001–2002 season.[52]

The major television networks have introduced and reinforced the notion that Arabs and Muslims equal terrorists. CBS televised a movie in 2002, *The President's Man: A Line in the Sand,* that included sinister Arab Muslims trying to use a nuclear bomb to blow up Texas. On *JAG* (1995–present),

Arab Muslims planted a bomb in an American school in the Middle East. On *The Agency* (2001–2003), Arab Muslim terrorists destroyed a department store in London, killing thousands. Middle Easterners are prevalently portrayed as part of a lunatic fringe in America.[53]

A *Seinfeld* character, the Soup Nazi, was based on one real live Al Yeganeh, who sells soup in a popular, tiny New York shop. He displays the stereotypical attitude of New York cabbies, often from the Middle East. A new 2003 program, *Whoopi,* featuring Whoopi Goldberg, includes a Persian character named Nasim who is employed at a hotel's front desk. He's referred to as an Arab, and although he points out the error, the scene ends with him singing a Middle Eastern tune and "walking like an Egyptian." *Whoopi* (the show) promotes negative stereotypes and paranoia in viewers. In effect, it encourages viewers to lump all Middle Easterners into a negative Arab identity.[54]

In the Disney movie, *Aladdin*, evil-looking Middle Easterners play the villains, while the heroes look and act like Europeans.[55] The opening song is racist, referring to a land, "Where they cut off your ear/If they don't like your face." Furthermore, the Middle Eastern characters are grotesque, and the bad guys have huge noses and exaggerated accents and wave swords around.[56]

Sadly, these stereotypes affect Americans of Middle Eastern descent. Children, in particular, become fearful and many hide their identities, claiming to be Spanish or Italian rather than an Arab. Many refuse to speak the Arabic language.[57]

People with Disabilities

Gail Williamson coordinates efforts to increase acting opportunities for the disabled through the office of Media Access. She also has a son with Down's syndrome. She praises the 1990s show *Life Goes On* (1989–1993), explaining that the show not only provided her son with a role model, it also educated viewers about Down's syndrome. She said that before the show was on, people would talk to her son through his parents. But after the show, people began to talk to him directly. She hopes that TV portrayals of people with disabilities can make that difference in other people's lives.[58]

Although 54 million Americans suffer from some type of disability, they are still a rarity on television. Following the NAACP's criticism of the industry for the lack of characters from ethnic minorities, the networks improved the ethnic diversity of television characters. However, advocates for the disabled lament that the disabled were not even mentioned in the 1999 diversity initiatives of the networks.[59]

Advocates for talent with disabilities say it is important that disabled characters not be the central story line; rather, actors prize supporting roles, in which the disability is a side issue to the plot. They cite Robert David Hall, who uses artificial legs following a truck collision, as a good example. He has played a coroner on *C.S.I.* (2000–present), and has played a judge on both *The Practice* (1999–2002) and *Family Law* (1999–2002).[60]

Too often, advocates claim, the media stereotype of the disabled, as villains, victims or "supercrips." They cite evil characters like the less-than-four-foot-tall Dr. Loveless, who created terror on a TV show, *Wild Wild West* (1965–1969), and the one-armed man hunted for as the real killer on *The Fugitive* (1963–1967). These kinds of characters allow viewers to blame the disabled as deserving his or her fate.

The disabled can also become the object of pity. Critics have attacked Jerry Lewis' portrayal of the disabled in his annual telethons, describing the portrayal as too sentimental. Advocates also object to the "supercrip"—Raymond Burr as the paraplegic homicide detective on *Ironside* (1967–1993). These characters tend to diminish the worth of the disabled by suggesting that the lives of the normal, not so heroic disabled are not good enough. It also undermines the attention that society needs to pay to issues of access, transportation and jobs for the disabled.[61]

Critics note that healthy, three-dimensional portrayals of the disabled existed in 1980s shows, such as *The Facts of Life* (1979–1988), in which Geri Jewell, an actress with cerebral palsy, was a regular character, as well as the Down syndrome teen in *Life Goes On.* In the 1990s disabled characters appeared less often than in the 1980s, but in the 2000s they have a greater presence than in the 1990s.

Marlee Matlin, who is deaf, plays a regular character on *The West Wing,* and *Malcolm in the Middle* features Malcolm's friend, Stevie, a severely asthmatic boy who uses a wheelchair. Matlin's character deals with her high-powered job, as well as the complications of courtship with Josh Lyman with an interpreter always present. Stevie deals with the issues typical to 10-year-olds, such as becoming independent from his mother and joining in Malcolm's mischief. Advocates for the disabled praise these characters for showing the disabled as "normalized." They are people dealing with the problems of everyday life, just like the able-bodied.[62]

Activists for the disabled are also urging industry producers to use more disabled actors in the roles of disabled people. Laura Innes, the actress who plays the disabled Dr. Kerry Weaver on *ER* (1994–present), doesn't use a crutch or even a cane in real life. Actress Christopher Templeton uses a cane in real life because she had polio as a child. She auditioned for the part, but did not get it. Perhaps she just wasn't right for the part, but the disabled community gave *ER* a lot of flak for the choice. Since then, *ER* takes great pains to include the disabled in its repertory of actors.[63]

The disabled community also credits Christopher Reeve's response to his spinal cord injury, incurred while jumping his horse, with bringing positive attention to the disabled. He appeared at speaking engagements and worked to raise awareness and funding for research into spinal cord injuries, as well as other disabilities.

Ageism in the Media

Tyne Daly, as Maxine Gray on *Judging Amy*, exemplifies the rare older character on TV who has a three-dimensional personality, a career and even a sex life. More commonly, older characters, like the grandmother on *Malcolm in the Middle* and the Barones on *Everybody Loves Raymond* interfere with and annoy the younger characters. The Barones, who live across the street from Ray and his wife, think nothing of walking into Ray's house without knocking.[64] If older characters aren't meddling, they dodder in nursing homes, being spoon-fed.[65]

Even more commonly, older characters simply do not exist on TV. While people 65 and older make up 13 percent of the population, prime time television portrays only 2 percent of characters as age 65 and over.[66] In addition, less than 10 percent of the older characters on prime time have main roles. Also, they aren't usually shown in loving relationships. Especially in sitcoms, the elderly are shown as negative, opinionated, burdens.[67] And while more than half of the older U.S. population is female, older women in main roles on television are much scarcer than older men.[68] In fact, three senior male actors at a conference of senior citizens charged that women over age 40 are considered "taboo," and not desireable actresses. They noted that even Meryl Streep suffers from ageism.[69] Indeed, in 2000, all the major female characters in their 40s were off the air—Murphy Brown, Ellen, Roseanne and Cybill were all gone.

The roles elderly women do play tend to be associated with family and to be family motivated. Older men tend to be more independent than older female characters, not necessarily driven by family. However, in general, the elderly are not shown as effective in dealing with problems compared to younger characters and these portrayals do not reflect the real lives of older people.[70] Given the importance of television as a provider of role models for behavior, there is little available for viewers to use to help them age.[71]

—What You Can Do—

- As your children watch TV, ask them about the portrayals of girls and women. What kind of occupations do they have? Are the portrayals stereotypically sexist? Do the women obsess about finding a man? Talk about whether you think the models are good ones for kids to imitate.

- If your children watch shows like *The Powerpuff Girls*, discuss the problems of the presence of violence and aggression. Perhaps what is being marketed as "strong" female characters is really no better than violence in general.

- If you don't currently have Nickelodeon, give serious thought to getting it. Nickelodeon's strong female characters include healthy ones on *Clarissa Explains it All*, *The Secret World of Alex Mack* and *The Mystery Files of Shelby Woo*. Nickelodeon also features shows with diverse ethnicities—Dora, the explorer, is Latina, and Shelby Woo is Asian-American, for example. At the same time, not everything on Nickelodeon is good. The rude behavior on shows like *Spongebob Squarepants* is not good for kids.

- Most girls feel good about themselves through elementary school. But in junior high and high school, their self-esteem drops, largely due to the unrealistic images of females in the media. Keep this in mind and reinforce the things your girls do well.

- If your girls like computer games, work to search out those that feature active female characters. Avoid games like Cosmopolitan Virtual Makeover and Barbie Fashion Designer, which promote sexist stereotypes.

- Reexamine the collection of animated Disney movies

you own. Watch them critically looking for stereotypical characters. There are probably many that you should not let your children watch.

• Watch TV with your children and discuss the portrayal of male characters. Are they violent or macho? What kinds of jobs do they have? Are they obsessed with sex? Discuss whether or not you think these are healthy models for boys.

• Reassure your children that the portrayals of women and men on TV are not necessarily realistic and need not be imitated.

• Actively seek out programming that features characters from diverse backgrounds and encourage your children to watch them. Look for programs that feature relationships between diverse people. *Sesame Street* is an excellent example. Other programs with racial diversity include *That's So Raven*, starring Raven-Symone, the youngest child on *The Cosby Show* which is on the Disney Channel. *Scout Safari*, on NBC is set in South Africa and features a White girl named Scout and her best friend Bongani, a young Black man, and often addresses the issues of post-apartheid South Africa. The current series of *Zoom* includes kids who are White, Black, Hispanic and Asian. And *Barney* features not only racially diverse kids, it includes kids with various disabilities, including a character who uses sign language.

• Look for programs to watch in which minority characters have main roles and a variety of occupations.

• If you see characters with disabilities on television, discuss them with your children. Perhaps students at their schools have disabilities. Discuss with them how

TV's portrayals compare to real life.

- Examine the portrayals of older characters on TV. Discuss with your children how they compare to the older people your children know, especially older women.

Chapter 6

Why Ernie Doesn't Read:

The Media and Your Child's Brain

In 1993, Lisa heard about the plight of thousands of Romanian orphans and went to Romania to try to rescue some of them. She brought home a six-year-old girl named Magda, and that summer she brought the little girl to the annual family reunion.

Magda and her story were heartbreaking. The child had been confined to a crib for her entire life. She couldn't stand or walk, so Lisa wheeled her around in a stroller. Because Magda had never eaten solid food, Lisa chopped chicken into tiny bits and mixed it with mashed potatoes to feed her. Magda was not toilet trained. She didn't talk. Even though Lisa gave the little girl the best medical and psychological care available, she wasn't able to make up for Magda's missing that critical "window" of development.

Although Magda's lack of development was clearly not related in any way to media use, her story illustrates how lack of stimulation at critical periods cannot be corrected. Certain age periods are ripe for certain developmental tasks, such as language and speech acquisition, and crawling and walking. For example, a child confined to a body cast during the first four years of life will eventually learn to walk, but it will not be the smooth walk of unconfined children.[1]

How The Brain Develops

When babies are born, their brains are filled with trillions of neurons waiting to be programmed. By the age of eight months, 1,000 trillion connections called synapses have been created.[2] During the first three to four years of life, the experiences of childhood "wire" the brain. The brain acquires structure from the sound of rain on the roof, the feel of sand in a sandbox, the colors of the fruits and vegetables in the produce department of the grocery store, and the relationships with parents, siblings and others. In order to promote this wiring, children need physical activity, exposure to language as spoken by real live people, and experiences in the real three-dimensional world.[3] They need interaction with their parents and time for spontaneous, free play. The brain continues its wiring process until about age 10. Then the brain begins discarding the synapses that have gotten the least use and keeping those that have been used through life experiences.[4]

If your children are getting "simulated" reality from television, film and computers, rather than real-life experiences, they risk lack of development of the pre-frontal cortex of the brain. This part of the brain controls thinking, learning, self-control and the ability to pay attention.[5] One scientific study measured the activity of the frontal cortex using functional Magnetic Resonance Imaging (fMRI). The test measures activity in various parts of the brain and takes second-by-second pictures of the activity so that researchers have a visual image of what parts of the brain are being activated. In this study, researchers used one group of "normal" adolescents and one group of adolescents diagnosed with Disruptive Behavioral Disorder (DBD). The two groups were matched according to how much violent media and video games they had been exposed to during the previous year. All of the adolescents were asked to perform mathematical and word association tasks, and while they did these, their brain functions were assessed using the fMRI. Researchers found a relationship between exposure to media violence and brain function. That is, kids who had had more exposure to violent media had less activity in the frontal cortex compared to kids who'd had less exposure to violent media. The exposure to media violence slows down the development of the thinking, reasoning and emotional control areas of the brain.[6]

Another part of the brain, the amygdala, produces aggression and deals with matters of fear. Its responses are controlled by the emotional cortex. If the emotional cortex is not developed by emotional stimulation or is somehow traumatized, children do not feel normal emotions or they may respond inappropriately in certain situations. They experience more fear and rage than children with normally developed emotional cortexes and may be unable to control aggressive impulses.[7]

For healthy brain development, kids need three to four hours of vigorous activity and interaction with their peers a day.[8] Presently, kids' exposure to TV, DVD's, computers, computer games and the Internet (total "screen time") is now an average of 4½ hours daily. Combined with the hours kids spend in school, this amount could seriously cut into the time available for vigorous activity and time with friends.[9]

These developmental concerns are so serious that the American Academy of Pediatrics has recommended that children under age two should not have any exposure to television. They decry the development of *Teletubbies*, created for one-year-olds,[10] and *Sesame Street's* makeover designed to appeal to two-year-olds.[11] While the AAP's recommendations apply specifically to TV, other problematic video sources include videos and DVDs, such as *Baby Einstein*.

Problems with Screen Immersion

What are the consequences of this unprecedented immersion in screens?

One consequence involves the attention span. Most experienced teachers will tell you that students' attention spans have decreased over the years. In addition to short attention spans, this exposure is related to disruptive behavior and an unwillingness or inability to stick with challenging tasks.[12] A number of researchers maintain that heavy screen use is linked to attention deficit disorder (ADD). They argue that heavy exposure causes over-stimulation of the brain from the rapid-fire changes of images, the fast pans and zooms, the rapid intercutting of shots, the quick movements and the special effects. The result is a short attention span and hyperactivity. One psychiatrist has argued that the hyperactive child has been conditioned by television to prefer rapid-fire changes in images and is trying to recreate this "flickering."[13]

Another result appears to be difficulty with language development. We've all applauded as a two-year-old flawlessly sings the jingle for a fast food restaurant or a breakfast cereal, but just because the child can sing the jingle doesn't mean he or she understands the words. For example, I remember learning to sing "Gladly the Cross I'd Bear" in Sunday School, and then asking my mom, "What does a cross-eyed bear have to do with church?" Language develops as kids talk one on one with a parent or caregiver. They need to actually use language and get feedback from a real live person. When kids watch TV, they aren't really using language. They hear it, but don't quite process it because the visual images are so much more powerful than the words.[14] In fact, in homes where the TV is on all the time, rather like "white noise," the speech development of children is significantly delayed. The constant background noise keeps them from learning to talk. And children whose speech development is behind at age three are destined for lifelong problems in school.[15]

Another important developmental task of childhood is learning to read. Babies learn to develop relationships with books beginning with "mouthing" board books. They proceed to holding books, turning pages and turning books upright.[16] Studies about how children learn to read also conclude that before they actually learn to read, they need to learn that being able to read is important. Many excellent children's programs teach such things as vocabulary, phonics, blending and rhyming. But whether or not these shows address the importance of the skill is not known. One disturbing study of *Sesame Street* found that while the show successfully teaches children to identify letters and numbers, it does little or nothing to teach children the value of literacy. An analysis of 350 segments of *Sesame Street* found only two segments that focused on the usefulness of reading. Further, there were only nine examples of characters reading even in the background. Bob, for example, read the paper while waiting for a bus, and Bert read a cookbook. Additionally, there were only 21 segments that included print on the set, such as street signs or cereal boxes. Given the inner city location of the street, one could surely expect to see advertising signs, logos or graffiti.

In addition, there were examples in which a Muppet's attempts to read were undermined. For example, in one segment Grover was a waiter, but rather than write down a patron's order, he played rhyming games to remember the order. He failed to bring the right food to the patron, who repeatedly suggested that he write down the order, but Grover didn't. The frustration of the patron could have been used to demonstrate the value of reading and writing, but it wasn't.

In another example, Grover was a taxi driver, and his customer wanted to go to the library. Grover worked to convince the customer to go somewhere else—to the zoo or a movie. Another missed opportunity to teach kids to value reading. The authors concluded that to encourage children to want to learn to read, children must see reading as a valued and useful activity, which it presently is not on *Sesame Street.*[17]

Other studies conclude that kids don't read because they don't practice reading. Mastering reading is hard work and takes several years. In contrast, the media do not require literacy in order to enjoy them, and many kids take the easy way out. Even in school, mastering reading is not the necessity it was in an earlier time.

Helen, who teaches high school English in one of the most highly regarded school districts in the nation, told me that she always introduces a literary work with the video. For example, the study of *Romeo and Juliet* is preceded by viewing the 1996 movie starring Claire Danes and Leonardo DiCaprio. This version of the classic takes place in the fantasy Verona Beach just outside of Los Angeles and features the Montagues and Capulets as mobsters and street thugs.

Romeo and Juliet are MTV street kids dressed in futuristic costumes, who tote guns rather than swords and drive convertibles rather than horses. Having seen this movie surely makes it difficult for readers to imagine their own versions of *Romeo and Juliet.* They may be confused by the other characters and scenes in Shakespeare's play. In truth, the video in advance likely compromises the students' appreciation of Shakespeare's story.

The Necessity of Play

Heavy media use also displaces activities of childhood that are necessary for developing good interpersonal relationships. One such activity is "play"—especially outdoor play. Up until the mid 1970s, kids spent most of their free time outdoors, perhaps just "hanging out," but not watching television. Since the mid 1980s our children have primarily been raised indoors, where watching television is much more likely to be the activity.[18] In addition, the play in which kids do engage often consists of organized activities into which their parents have enrolled them—tennis lessons, Little League Baseball, soccer teams.

When I was a kid, my buddies in the neighborhood and I played pick-up softball games in the alley—we improvised the rules, depending on how many kids we had and how good they were. We also made tents out of our mothers' old bedspreads and the small painted rocks that edged our moms' gardens. We pinned two bedspreads to our clothes line, pulled out the bottom edges and weighted the edges with rocks. We then had an A-frame tent, and the big excitement was to get a picnic lunch and eat it in the tent we had made ourselves. Currently, kids' heavy use of the media pushes a lot of spontaneous play out of their days.

Parents also need to play with their children. One child psychologist has asserted that parents don't play with their children because they didn't have parents who played with them.[19] Parents and kids need to play with clay, go to parks, and play in sand and dirt. When our daughters were young, they helped their dad plant seeds in the vegetable garden by playing a game called, "hiding the seeds from the giants." Nowadays, I hear mothers talking about the "play dates" their children have, rather than casually meeting up with kids on the block. Again, what kids need is unstructured play rather than the organized play into which so many kids are booked.

Another activity that gets edged out by the media is family interaction. If the TV is on during meals and after supper, communication between family members is less likely to occur. And slipping into the passive retreat of TV allows kids to suppress their problems and anxieties, and avoid working them out.

Computers and Development

In addition to television, computers impede brain development. The folks at Apple and Microsoft have been geniuses at convincing parents that children need computers. Indeed, in 1999, 70 percent of American homes had personal computers.[20] Parents get suckered into software for their preschoolers that advertises it as a way to make their children smarter. Marketers target even babies with a product called "lapware." To use "lapware,"the baby must sit on a lap and have his or her finger held and made to click the mouse. Is mouse-clicking a useful skill for a baby to develop? Indeed, *Jump Start Baby* and *Reader Rabbit's Playtime for Babies* are just two examples of the myriad computer software products designed for children aged nine to 24 months.

However, educational psychologist Jane Healy maintains that children under age seven should not be using computers at all.

Julie, a Professor of Statistics, enrolled her son in a private school that doesn't use computers to teach math concepts. Although she uses computers and technology in her profession, she wanted to make sure that her son learned the principles of addition and subtraction before he began punching numbers in on a calculator. Healy further explains that children need to learn in a three-dimensional world, making use of all of their senses. Furthermore, she claims that computer use impedes a child's ability to think logically, pay attention and develop memory skills. Computers isolate kids, when what they need is interaction with other people.

Computers can also hinder creativity and the development of the imagination. Kids who draw using computers don't want to draw with markers because their pictures aren't as perfect as the computer drawings.[21] Six-year-old Sally loves the Disney movie, *Cinderella*. But rather than drawing pictures of scenes from the movie, she showed me her Cinderella software. The opening screen pictured the outdoor setting of the movie. When Sally clicked on a window in the castle we moved to a room inside. When we got to the empty parlor, various pieces of furniture appeared at the bottom of the screen. Sally clicked and dragged the pieces she wanted and placed them in the room. She created a picture that was a perfect replica of a scene from the movie, not her own version of the story.

Pressure on Schools

Schools have also been seduced into the technology world. One professor of education described the high-pressure marketing tactics of the computer industry as a "mega-scam" forcing schools to forgo necessary items like textbooks to get computers.[22] Indeed, the pledge by former President Clinton and Vice President Gore that every classroom be on-line made the push for technology irresistible. School boards made the move to acquire technology a top priority. When a survey was released that showed California was 45th in the nation in terms of students' access to technology, alarm bells went off and then-Governor Pete Wilson pledged to spend $500 million on technology to assure that California high school graduates have the skills needed to compete in the job market.[23]

Vendors often woo school officials by inviting them to all-expenses-paid conferences in attractive places like Aspen and New Orleans. One superintendent who chose not to attend such a conference explained that it becomes difficult to resist the vendors' pressure to get attendees to commit to their products. Marketers also frequently hire former superintendents as consultants to help create effective sales pitches targeted to other superintendents.[24] Additionally, the donation of computers to schools by e.g., Apple, resembles a Trojan Horse—once inside the fortress, victory is inevitable. If Apple has in-roads into your child's school, what upgrades of software and hardware do you suppose will be bought? And when students have successfully persuaded you that they need a personal computer at home, what brand do you suppose they'll want?

This head-long plunge into technology has occurred with little careful examination of its value. Healy said she talked to one computer salesman at a technology conference exhibit. She asked him if he'd tell her why she should use the computer instead of "regular materials—you know, books, pencils, teachers?" He said he hadn't thought about that and that of the several thousand educators he had talked to, no one had ever asked him that question before.[25]

Educational Outcomes

The results of the technology in schools have not been impressive. Healy noted that the teachers she interviewed found that 85 percent of the software in schools was worthless and some of it damaging. For example, the creativity scores of students using computers for reading readiness dropped 50 percent. In addition, educators said that computer learning deprives children of the human environments needed for healthy social and emotional development.

Another negative is that computers emphasize passive learning that retards kids' development as powerful learners.[26] Healy claimed that too often the software was chosen by "techie"people who knew little about education and tended to pick software because it was "cute."[27] Furthermore, the results in terms of students' school performance have not been notable.

Studies that did find a gain in achievement were of student performance when computers were used for higher order learning such as simulations. One study described a complex simulation related to the concept of velocity, using the varying speeds of elevators floor by floor as an example.[28]

However, there is no evidence that this type of complex simulation, created by researchers at the University of Massachusetts Dartmouth, is widely used by educators, so the benefits of the computer in most educational situations are debatable.

Other researchers note that most studies that find gains in achievement are not careful scientific studies and that many of those studies were funded by the computer industry, making the results suspect.[29] Many studies of performance show no appreciable gains in achievement from using computers in schools. In fact, two national studies reported in 1997 found no differences in students' performances on standardized tests between those in the most technologically advanced schools compared to those without technology.[30]

In addition to finding minimal, if any, gains in achievement, many educators lament that the primary use of computers has been to "drill and kill," a reference to their use to teach basic math facts, spelling and vocabulary—essentially extremely expensive flash cards.[31]

Additional Problems for Schools

In addition to unimpressive educational results, there are other problems associated with computers in schools. One, obviously, is the high cost. In 1997, schools nationwide spent four billion dollars on computer technology, and that is a miniscule amount compared to the money it will take to get computers into all schools.[32] Furthermore, as soon as a computer is turned on, it is obsolete and in line for replacement.

Critics also decry the absence of adequate teacher training in how to best teach with computers. Only 15 percent of teachers have what *Forbes* called adequate training in how to use computers in their classrooms.[33] Most teachers receive training at workshops that sometimes last only an afternoon. Others are self-taught or rely on the help of their colleagues to figure out what to do with the technology. Complex software is difficult to use to effectively enhance the curriculum. Perhaps that's why so much computer use is devoted to drills.

When computers crash, there is far too little technical support for teachers. Most teachers are not also engineers, and with minimal technical support, computers can be "down" for weeks. One principal finally simply shut down her computer lab because she couldn't get adequate technical support.[34]

To complicate matters, there is little agreement on how best to use technology. The move to acquire it was driven by "techno-reformers, mostly public officials, corporate leaders, and other non-educators far removed from classrooms."[35] These reformers ignored the fact that teaching is not like factory work that lends itself to automation and technology. Computers may go the way of other "cutting edge" boondoggles, such as programmed learning, an incredibly boring and time-consuming learning device, or closed circuit television systems that have little or no programming.

Further, the addition of technology has often forced out other beneficial aspects of the curriculum. In the book *High Tech Heretic* (Anchor, 2000), Clifford Stoll described his visits to computer labs in schools in California. He would ask the principals what the labs used to be. He was upset to learn that computer labs had displaced music studios, art rooms and libraries. Because of the new lack of space, music and art were no longer taught, and the schools had gotten rid of the books that used to make their homes in the library.[36]

The Art of Teaching

Teaching depends on the creation of a caring human relationship and strong emotional bonds between teacher and student.[37] Even Apple Computer's founder Steve Jobs, who gave massive numbers of computers to schools said:

"I've come to the inevitable conclusion that the problem (in education) is not one that technology can hope to solve. What's wrong with education cannot be fixed with technology. No amount of technology will make a dent."[38]

Teaching varies greatly from the kinds of manufacturing tasks that have been successfully automated. It's not like making a car, butchering cows or other jobs requiring the execution of repetitive tasks. The introduction of computers into teaching undermines the teacher's role as the authority figure and the importance of building relationships with students to help them learn. It eliminates the community created in a classroom and isolates students at machines. In an editorial in *Forbes,* the editor cited an internal memo from the Technology Editor, reminding fellow editors that "the best schools will eventually recognize a fact that's been apparent since Plato sat on [sic] Socrates knee: Education depends on the intimate contact between a good teacher—part performer, part dictator, part cajoler—and an inquiring student." Further, he predicted : *"In the end it is the poor who will be chained to the computer; the rich will get teachers."* [italics added] (156)[39]

—What You Can Do—

- Don't let your toddler watch much television. Just because someone is marketing programs for toddlers (e.g., *Teletubbies, Barney*) doesn't mean those programs are good for them.

- Limit children older than two years of age to no more than two hours of TV per day.

- Don't leave your TV set on unless someone is actually watching it. Kids need silence to give them time to reflect on their world and have conversations with you—a real live human being.

- Don't get your children on computers at a young age. Age seven is young enough. Just because some software is advertised for kids, doesn't mean it's good for them.

- Resist your school's efforts to plunge headlong into acquiring technology without adequate study of what it will do for your students. Share this chapter with school officials.

- Get board books for your babies. Let them chew on them. Show them how to turn pages and read aloud to them.

- Read to your children. Let them see you reading and placing a value on the skill.

- Spend time with your children in the real three-dimensional world. Play outdoors; talk and listen to them.

- Involve your children in household activities —let them help you set the table or fold laundry, for example, instead of turning on the TV to babysit them while you do these chores alone.

Chapter 7

"We've Gotta Have It Now!"

Commercials and Consumerism

Jonathon, a two-year-old, loves to spend time with his mom and his *Cheerios Counting Book.* It's a board book that's safe for toddlers to chew on as well as to learn about books. The editorial review from Amazon.com praises it and notes that on the last page the book urges the toddler to eat 20 O's when they're done counting. The review makes no mention of the fact that this is one form of advertising for Cheerios. His mother says she normally wouldn't buy a product that is actually advertising, but this book is so "cute" that it's irresistible.

Sarah's mother says the same thing about *The Sunmaid Raisin Book.* Sarah brings her the book when she wants a snack. Another mother describes the fun she and her daughter have counting, reading and eating raisins. The *Pepperidge Farm Goldfish Fun Book* promotes eating Goldfish to learn to count, but even the reviewers make no mention of the salt and fat content of the snack.

Interestingly, *The M&M'S Counting Board Book* is so popular with Marie's daughter that she always has a sack of M&M'S on hand. She doesn't have any reservations about the fat, sugar and caffeine content of the candy. Advertising in board books aimed at babies and toddlers is a relatively new phenomenon, and it's a clever way to capture the market of the very youngest consumers.

Indeed, parents and educators worry about kids' exposure to television advertising, and the scope of this exposure is alarming. Information prepared for a Congressional Briefing in 2003 reported that children see more than 40,000 television advertisements in one year![1] This figure does not include advertising on billboards, magazine ads, posters in school lunchrooms and other ads.

Kids' Purchasing Power

Advertisers know that kids, as a group, control vast sums of money, almost all of it expendable. The kid's market, six to 11-year-olds, spent $25 billion of their own money in 1999.[2] The "tween" market, defined as kids in third grade through middle school, spend $41 billion on themselves, according to a 2002 report.[3] A 2001 study reported that teens get and spend $55 billion that they get from their parents and even more money that teens earn from part-time jobs.[4] Georgia, who taught in a junior high in an affluent suburb in California, told me that some of her students' had allowances of several hundred dollars a week or more.

In addition to the money they spend on themselves, kids influence a great deal of family spending. In 1999, six- to 11-year-olds affected $187 billion of their parents' purchases.[5] The "tween" market has partial control of $260 billion of family purchases, according to a report published in 2002.[6] Indeed, kids influence nearly half of all of their family's purchasing decisions.[7] A 1999 survey of parents found that over 70 percent of them said they turned to their kids for advice about what computer to buy.[8] Cruise lines, designer clothes and even cars advertise to kids. Porsche is marketing to kids age six through 10 because they realize that kids determine what is "cool," and Porsche wants to be "cool." A recent teen targeted magazine ad for Mercedes featured teenage girls posed sulkily and telling readers that if their dads could buy a Mercedes, so could yours.[9]

Building Brand Loyalty

Ad agencies are beginning to target kids between the ages of birth and three years old because research shows kids understand brands at a very young age.[10] They also know that kids are insecure and that peers make judgments about them based on whether or not a kid has the right "stuff." Kids know what the right "stuff" is at a very early age. For instance, a woman in Michigan saw a young girl, about eight years old, in a store and commented that she really liked the child's outfit. The girl quickly replied that it was a Donna Karan. Advertisers are eager to establish their brand as the "right" brand, seeking loyalty in the very youngest consumers. They say "brand them when they're babies" and refer to the "drool factor," meaning that as babies drool they look down and see the brand of the clothes they are wearing.[11] Advertiser's goal is "cradle-to-grave" branding—they know that if they can win brand loyalty in the very young, they will have loyal consumers for many years.

Shopping Online

Once merchants figure out how to serve kids with Internet buying, kids' buying power will increase. Currently, most teens do not have a credit card, which prevents them from ordering online. Today's group of teenagers, called the NET Generation or Generation Y, is made up of 60 million kids, so getting these teens to buy online and develop brand loyalty is very attractive.[12] E-commerce companies have come up with several solutions to the problem. Parents can buy gift certificates at GiveAnything.com that allow a child to shop online. Teens can shop at a restricted set of online sites. They can't buy pizza or movie tickets, but they must spend the certificates on something tangible. They are not allowed to use "adult-only" sites, and parents can set spending limits.[13] Parents can also set up accounts using RocketCash, Flooz, DoughNET and iCanBuy.[14] In addition to giving teens access to online shopping, parents have the opportunity to teach their kids valuable lessons about careful shopping.

Parental Guilt and Nagging

Parental guilt fuels kids' buying power. In families with two working parents, kids often spend little time with Mom and Dad. In divorced families, kids see each parent less because they spend time with each one separately. Parents who feel guilty about the limited time they spend with their kids give their kids a great deal of pocket money. Parental guilt also improves a kid's chances of being successful at nagging for things. As any parent knows, today's kids have developed a powerful ability to nag. One survey found that if a parent says "no" to a purchase, 60 percent of kids will request the item nine times. Ten percent of kids 12 and 13 years old will ask more than 50 times for something they want. One nine-year-old said if he really wants something he is prepared to nag for it 150 times. Fifty-five percent of the kids say that more often than not they get their parents to cave in, and 60 percent said they had learned effective nagging techniques before they entered first grade.[15]

Interestingly, advertisers try to include ideas for nagging scripts in their ads, so that a kid can nag with a quality of importance in why they need the product. Nagging for Barbie's

Dream House is quite effective when a kid follows Mattel's advice, arguing that it's needed so Barbie and Ken can have a family. That's far superior to arguing that it's needed because it's pretty and pink.[16]

This combination of buying power, targeted marketing, effective nagging and "guilt money" creates some child-rearing problems. Sixty-eight percent of parents say their kids are spoiled and materialistic.[17] Furthermore, while 70 percent of parents surveyed think it's important to teach kids how to budget their money and spend wisely, only 28 percent say they've been successful at it.[18]

Television Advertising

Many parents assume that kids know a TV commercial when they see one and that they understand an advertiser's intent is to get them to buy something. However, many kids haven't figured that out. I conducted interviews with 40 fifth grade students enrolled in an upper-middle-class community in the Midwest. Most of them were 10 years old, and I wanted to find out how much they knew about TV commercials. When I asked them how they would explain a TV ad to a kindergartner, they commonly said they'd tell the kid it's an advertisement with no further explanation.

Next I asked them to explain what an advertisement was, and many of them weren't clear about the concept. About half said it was to get viewers to buy something, but the other half said it was simply to give viewers information about new products and where you could buy them.[19]

As psychologists know, many kids under the age of eight have trouble sorting fantasy from reality. Presumably, younger kids are even more vulnerable to TV commercials than the fifth graders in my study.

Even if a kid is savvy to the intent of commercials, he or she is still vulnerable to advertising. One strategy advertisers use is to prey on kids' insecurities about "fitting in" with their peers. Advertising tells children they are too fat, that they are losers or ugly, and that the way to solve their problems is to buy "stuff." They convince kids that if they don't have the right athletic shoes or designer clothes, they won't have friends. Kids believe their "stuff" defines who they are, and they say that having the right stuff makes them feel good about themselves.[20]

Advertisers take sophisticated steps to learn about the youth market. Researchers conduct focus groups with teens who are paid approximately $125 to participate and let their brains get picked about what is "cool." They even do "ethnographic" studies in which they talk to teens in their homes and bedrooms to get a feel for what can become "cool." Marketers call this "cool hunting." Advertisers hire teens to go into chat rooms and tout the desirability of certain products and hire college students to throw parties at which certain products will be served and used.[21]

Companies are willing to go to great lengths to get their products used by the "hippest" consumers. A firm called "SoulKool" gives new products to young adults who have been assessed for their "coolness" through an extensive questionnaire. These "cool" young adults, called "street teamers," then give new products to their friends, thereby associating "cool" with the new product. For example, "street teamers" gave out 60,000 coupons for trial memberships at Crunch workout clubs. Following the trial period, purchases of regular memberships soared. Depending on the product, street teamers may be paid to give away such things as CDs, posters, gear bags, stickers, tickets to concerts or raves.[22] At the end of 2002, SoulKool had a database of 20,000 names of "cool" people to whom they sent new products.[23]

Product Licensing

Product licensing also bombards kids with advertising. Hi-C juice teamed up with the Cartoon Network to feature characters such as the Powerpuff Girls on their juice boxes. Parents can buy children's underwear featuring Dora the Explorer, Barbie, SpongeBob, Spiderman and many more television characters. Even commercial-free PBS predicted licensing fees from their *Teletubbies* products would earn PBS $2 billion in revenue in 2000.[24] eBay offers more than 1,300 *Teletubbies* products for sale, including t-shirts, sneakers, backpacks, posters, goodie bags, Tinky Winky dolls, swim suits and much, much more. Over 4,000 *Sesame Street* products are available on eBay, including Cookie Monster cookie jars, a wide assortment of DVDs, monster puppets, clothes, music boxes, lunch boxes and many, many more licensed gizmos. The Muppets are featured in video games, and there are talking Ernie toys, *Sesame Street* saxophones and medical doctor's kits. In addition to earning licensing revenues, all of these products promote the TV shows.

Product Placement

Products are also hawked through product placement in films and television programs. With this strategy, a celebrity essentially "endorses" a product by using it, or it simply appears as a prop. Sales of Red Stripe beer increased over 50 percent after Tom Cruise drank it in *The Firm*. In *Deep Impact*, a character sips Avalon spring water; a *Seinfeld* episode featured Junior Mints; and *E.T.* enjoyed Reese's Pieces following M&M'S refusal to place their product in the hit film.[25] Companies usually have to pay for the placement. Subway and PepsiCo spent over $5 million for placement in Jim Carrey's *Ace Ventura: When Nature Calls*. Sometimes merchandise pays for placement. Ford appeared in *Jurassic*

Park for a "fee" of 10 Ford Explorers. Much of the movie *Bye Bye, Love* took place at McDonald's, and in return McDonald's loaned the movie the use of an authentic McDonald's set for the shooting.[26] An episode of *The West Wing* featured the Chinese restaurant, Panda Express, getting exposure to 20 million viewers.[27]

TiVo, and other devices that allow a viewer to cut out the commercials as a show is being watched, have spawned a new variation on product placement; a product is incorporated right into the show, eliminating the need for commercial interruptions. A character might be featured washing clothes and raving to another character about Tide, or the variety show set may be covered with posters for Pepsi.

Commercialism in Schools

Many school districts, facing the failure of school bond referenda and the consequent shortage of funds, have taken advantage of many commercial opportunities. Chris Whittle's Channel One, one of the first, requires students to watch a 12-minute, daily news program that includes two minutes of commercials. In return for this audience, Whittle gives schools free video equipment.[28] Schools also sell naming rights. Shell Oil sponsors a school in Oakland, California, called Shell Academy. The school got $2 million for giving that name to their school.[29] A school in New Jersey sold naming rights for the gymnasium to ShopRite grocery store—it's now ShopRite of Brooklawn Gymnasium.[30] In Arizona, Wells Fargo bought the naming rights to a high school athletic conference for $12,000.[31]

Schools sell the naming rights to auditoriums, music rooms, football fields and libraries, for example. Schools also sell "pouring rights." Commonly, Coke or Pepsi pays a school up to $100,000 a year to have exclusive rights to sell their brands of soft drinks in the school. Usually the school has a quota that must be sold, which results in administrators urging teachers to let their students drink Coke during class, allowing access to the vending machines during lunch periods, even in states where it's against the law.[32]

Many school districts plaster ads on the sides of school buses. A school bus in Colorado Springs, Colorado, covered in ads for Burger King and Wendy's, shocked a mother who was walking her eight-year-old daughter to the school bus stop.[33] In Denver, the schools partnered with Sunkist to develop health curriculum materials. Sunkist gave the money to develop the materials. In exchange, the school gave space for Sunkist's advertising campaign called, "Just One—A Whole Day's Vitamin C" on school buses, sports scoreboards and brochures.[34]

Indeed, advertiser-generated curriculum materials smack of commercialism. Pepsi worked on the development of a science course called, "The Carbonated Beverage Company." Students do taste tests on soft drinks, analyze the products and tour the local Pepsi plant. Math books use Tootsie Rolls to teach math concepts, and business courses use McDonald's restaurants as examples of how businesses are run.[35] Campbell's Soup provides an experiment for science classes in which students compare Campbell's Prego and Unilever's Ragu spaghetti sauces in terms of thickness. Not surprisingly, Campbell's is thicker. General Mills offers an experiment in which students compare the sensation of Fruit Gushers in the mouth to volcanic activity.[36] Oil companies supply curriculum materials about ecology and fast food restaurants provide guidelines about nutrition.[37]

Images of Pokemon and Pillsbury cookies cover cafeteria menus; Ads for Kellogg's Pop-Tarts and celebrities from Fox Broadcasting Company shows decorate school planners.[38] In 2000, Philip Morris created controversy by giving away 13 million textbook covers that featured a snowboarder and the words, "Don't Wipe Out. Think. Don't Smoke." However, students in Meza, Arizona, observed that the snowboard bore a remarkable resemblance to a lighted cigarette, and the students and their teacher organized a press conference to call attention to the image. They successfully got school officials to recall the book covers. In some places, Nike, Reebok, Adidas and others give shoes to top athletes—some schools are even referred to as "shoe schools."[39] The shoe companies get free advertising every time an athlete wears their shoes. One school tore up its basketball court to redo it with the names of ten corporate sponsors on the floor for 10,000 dollars each.[40]

Another school-related gimmick has been developed by a company called "Cunning Stunts." They pay well-dressed, attractive, sexy, college students to wear brand-name logos on their foreheads. The logos are applied by a transfer process, not tattoed, but the logo will last several weeks. Students are paid approximately $7 an hour to appear in public places for at least three hours daily.[41]

Fundraising programs that encourage buying from certain stores or certain brand names also commercialize schools. In my community Campbell's soup labels are collected in return for school equipment. Swiss Valley Dairy offers money to schools for collecting the caps from milk containers. Organizations such as a pre-school can team up with a grocery store for a "Shop and Save" set of days. If you shop on those days and give your receipts to the school, the grocery store will donate to your school. General Mills donates money for box tops from General Mills' products that students turn in. Merchants registered with an online company by the name of eScrip and contribute to the group you choose every time you use a credit or debit card registered with eScrip. Schoolpop offers similar deals. While at first glance these may look like philanthropic and harmless activities, they actually encourage shopping for certain brands and/or at certain stores.

Incentive programs also benefit businesses. For instance, Pizza Hut's "Book-It" promotion awards coupons for pizza to students who read a certain number of books.[42] Similarly, McDonald's "All-American Reading Challenge" gives coupons for burgers for reading books.[43]

All of these forms of commercialism, including the fundraising and incentive programs, create brand loyalty beginning at an early age. If you've been bringing Campbell's soup labels to school for 13 years, what brand of soup do you suppose you'll choose for your family?

The Price We Pay

This widespread consumerism creates serious problems. At the end of 2000 American household debt exceeded $7 trillion, and in that year Americans charged more than a trillion dollars on credit cards.[44] Some of this does get paid off, of course. However, in 2002 American households owed 101 percent of their income, up from 84 percent in 1992.[45] This means that virtually no one is saving money nowadays. As recently as 1996, households saved 5 percent of their income.[46] In terms of teens and young adults, debt looms as a huge problem. Currently, over half of young people between 16 and 22 years of age have credit cards. The 78 percent of college students who have at least one card, on average, owe nearly $3,000 and collectively account for nearly $150 billion of credit card debt.[47]

Many people can't figure out how to cope with their massive debt, so they declare bankruptcy. According to the American Bankruptcy Institute, over 1,200,000 Americans declared bankruptcy in 2000.[48] Further, in the population under 35 years of age, 461,000 went bankrupt in 1999.[49]

In addition to the negative financial implications of all of this commercialism and consumerism, consider the insecurities created in kids who have been told from a very young age that they are inadequate (too fat, too ugly, too "uncool"). This propaganda about inadequacy, especially for teens, for whom insecurity and awkwardness is part of the natural state of affairs, will create psychological and emotional problems.

—What You Can Do—

- Talk to your children about the purpose of advertising. Do it while you are watching commercials. Make it clear that advertising is trying to get you to buy something and that it is different from a television program.

- Talk with them about how the ad *wants* you to feel. Discuss whether buying the product in the ad will really deliver on its suggestion. Will you have more friends if you buy a certain video game, for example?

- Explain the concept of brand loyalty and how foolish it is. Take your children with you shopping and show them how to evaluate choices of food products, for example. If the generic or store brand has the same ingredients as the brand name, ask your child if there is any reason to select the brand name.

- If your children like to shop online, don't just give them your credit card number and let them buy. Children can write down your credit card information and use it when you are not present. Use one of the online gift certificates that restrict your children's access to "adult" sites.

- It's often difficult to resist licensed products, but do discuss with your children that these items—lunch boxes, pajamas, t-shirts—are advertising the featured program.

- Explain the notion of product placement. Watch a video or television program with your children and help them spot the placements.

- Work to develop policies about the commercialism in

your children's schools. Contact the Center for
Commercial-Free Public Education, get their surveys
and arrange for parent-teacher walk-throughs of your
children's schools. These allow parents and teachers
to judge how much commercialism there is in a school.

- Explain to your children how even the seemingly
positive "Shop and Save" type days at grocery stores
are really marketing ploys.

- Also explain how incentive programs (e.g. pizza coupons
for reading books) are really marketing gimmicks.

Chapter 8

Hit Men and Hookers:

Video Games in Your Child's Life *

Mandy works part time at a Blockbuster Video store in a small town in Wisconsin. She and her manager watched as many parents checked out "M" rated (age 17 and over) video games with their 10- to 12-year-old children. The "M" rating indicates that the game contains extreme violence, and may contain "mature" sexual themes and language, and is inappropriate for kids under age 17. When the parents got home and saw the nature of the games, they called the store to complain that the employees had wrongly rented "M" rated video games to their kids. In frustration, the manager put a hidden video camera in the "M" rated section of the video games. When parents complained, the manager invited them to come in to watch themselves help their kids rent the "M" rated games. Mandy's story is not unusual. Indeed, 90 percent of parents don't pay attention to the ratings on games their kids want to buy or rent.[1]

The "M" category of game raises the most controversy

---

*In this chapter, the term "video game" refers to computer and console games, as well.

about the industry. The Entertainment Software Rating Board describes "EC" (early childhood) games as appropriate for kids three and older. The "E" (everyone) games are suitable for gamers six and older. The "T" (teen) category of game may contain violence and suggestive themes, appropriate for gamers 13 years of age and older. "M" (mature) titles may include extreme violence and sexual content, suitable for kids over age 17. The "AO" (adults only) games may include graphic displays of violence and sex, and are appropriate only for gamers over age 18. However, the rating system has flaws. For example, one study found that 60 percent of games rated "E" (suitable for children as young as six years old) featured what was termed "significant" amounts of violent content.[2]

Moreover, the gaming industry flouts the rating system. For example, although Duke Nukem is rated "M," the marketing of Duke Nukem action figures to kids under the age of eight suggests that the company is aggressively targeting kids much younger than 17 years old.[3]

Additionally, the video game industry challenges the existence of a rating system and restrictions on what kids can rent. In 2003, a federal court in St. Louis found a law that restricted what kids can rent to be a violation of the First Amendment. The video game industry successfully argued that video games deserve the same protection as books, music, art and films. In 2001, a federal court ruled against a similar law in Indianapolis. The Governor of Washington approved a restriction on video game rentals, but the gaming industry plans to challenge that provision on free speech grounds as well.[4]

In places where restrictions do exist, game renters often fail to check kids' identification. Two 14-year-old Canadian boys successfully rented "M" games from every store they tried, with no trouble.[5] Additionally, a sting operation conducted by the Federal Trade Commission in 2001 found that 78 percent of kids under age 17 easily purchased "M" rated games,[6] and 67 percent of seven-year-old kids bought "M" rated games without trouble.[7]

Some types of video games are family oriented and appropriate for younger children—sports games, non-violent simulations, game shows and puzzle games, for example. However, the mature-rated video games make up the fastest growing share of the market, and the ones critics worry about most.[8] They object to the extensive horrific violence as well as the misogynistic representations of women.

Violence in Games

Critics disapprove of not only the amount of violence, but also the realistic and graphic nature of it. These games feature lifelike characters, close shots of the grotesque violence, realistic and ghoulish music and sound effects.[9] Much of the violence is grisly and perverse. One player marveled at the detail and reality of the gore and gruesomeness of Goldeneye 64, and speculated with awe at how much time must have gone into the creation of such a game.[10] In various versions of Mortal Kombat, players decapitate the enemies, pull out their spines, stomp on and squish their heads. If you kill someone with a chainsaw, blood spurts from the victim, covering the screen in a shower of blood. Blood is everywhere, wounds bleed for a long time, and victims often leave bloody footprints as they attempt to escape. Characters can burn their enemies and hear their agonizing screams, blow heads off and see blood spurt from their necks. They kill people with guns, hammers and meat cleavers.[11]

First Person Shooter Games

First-person-shooter games, in which the gamer is a character in the game are among the most popular. A gun barrel may appear in the lower portion of the screen, giving the appearance that the player shoots that gun. Although these games are rated "M," 50 percent of fourth graders choose first-person-shooter games as their favorites.[12] In the most popular games, the gamers are the bad guys. For example, in Grand Theft Auto III, the best-selling game in 2001,[13] players earn points by attacking innocent bystanders. In Grand Theft Auto: Vice City, one of the best-selling games in the world, players can have sex with a prostitute, then kill her and get their money back.[14]

Joysticks that are pistol grips that "kick" in the players' hands when they shoot enhance the sensation of killing. One ad for such a joystick proclaimed "'it is important to feel something when you kill.'"[15] Further, the technology has advanced to the point that shooters aim not at pixilated images of characters—rather the images are three dimensional and realistic. In addition, current computer technology is so fast, that it's called "real-time 3-D." Gamers roam at will in a three-dimensional, 360-degree setting. They are not restricted to predetermined movements like they are in games like Myst.[16]

First-person-shooter games result in excellent marksmanship. In one experiment, researchers compared the marksmanship of two groups of boys. One group of 20 boys had limited experience with first-person-shooter games and the other 20 were self-described as avid players of first-person-shooter games. The results shocked the researchers. The boys with limited experience hit the human silhouette targets 85 percent of the time and struck vital areas of the targets 75 percent of the time. The boys who were avid first-person-shooter game players hit the targets 99 percent of the time and struck vital areas 97 percent of the time. Their marksmanship rivaled those of highly qualified police officers![17]

Michael Carneal, the fourteen-year-old killer in Paducah, Kentucky, played first-person-shooter games for hundreds of hours. Although he had never before held a gun in his hand, he fired eight shots at students leaving a prayer meeting and got eight hits on eight different kids. He killed three of them with head shots, and paralyzed one. In total, he made five head shots and three on the upper body. His eight hits for eight shots compares to the average law enforcement officer who hits about one in five shots at a range of seven yards.[18]

Although critics of first-person-shooter games have tried unsuccessfully to connect them with the school shootings in the recent past, it seems likely that the school shooters would not have had the high success rate in killing without the skill learned from these games.

Violence Against Women

In addition to the graphic and realistic nature of the violence, games regularly feature violence against women. In fact, most games victimize women.[19] Grand Theft Auto: Vice City, for example, awards bonus points for killing a woman by kicking her to death. Shooters earn extra points for killing naked and tied up prostitutes and strippers who beg, "Kill me." Blood graphically spurts out of the women during the murders. In Grand Theft Auto III, gamers get bonus points for raping and then clubbing women to death. Gamers in Duke Nukem use pornographic posters of women for target practice.[20]

Consequences of Game Violence

Playing violent video games correlates with an increase in aggressive behavior. One study surveyed nearly 300 young adults about their use of video games and also their past delinquent behaviors. They found that the more time the subjects played violent video games the more likely they were to be aggressive and have participated in aggressive illegal behavior. Two hundred additional subjects played either a violent or a non-violent video game. After playing the game subjects were paired up and played a competitive game. If they won the game, they could blast their opponent with an offensive noise. The subjects who had played the violent video game prior to the competitive game play blasted their opponents longer and louder compared to those who had played the nonviolent video game. The researchers concluded that violent video game playing positively associates with increases in aggressive behavior.[21] In addition, a year-long study of 600 middle school children found that only 4 percent of kids who played no violent games got into fights while 38 percent of those who did play violent games got into fights.[22]

Researchers also believe that violence in video games is more powerful than watching television or film violence because games are interactive. Gamers don't just observe the violence, but rather create behavioral scripts and play out the violence.[23] Gamers' physiological responses to playing video games offer further evidence of the intense response game playing creates. One physician, who observed video gamers getting red-faced and agitated, conducted a test on his 10-year-old nephew. Before playing the game, the kid's heart rate was 90 beats per minute. But after just 10 minutes of playing Virtual Fighter IV, a game rated for teens, his heart rate approached 140 beats per minute and his blood pressure was sky-high at 186 over 121! The physician explained that a high level of arousal increases the likelihood that the player will learn that violent behavioral script, and learn that violence is a good way to solve problems.[24]

In addition to aggressive behavior, violent video games cause players to become desensitized to real life violence. This means that seeing it or using it doesn't bother them very much. In fact, these games teach kids to connect agony, torment and death with pleasure.[25] One appalled father described his preteen-aged son and a friend as they played Goldeneye 007, a game rated "T" for teens. As they cornered an opponent and killed him, blood splattered from the victim as he fell. The boys laughed with glee and "maniacal sneers" as they taunted the victim and shot him.[26] A player of Gold-eneye 64 sited his victim in the crosshairs of his weapon and shot the character in the back of the head. Then he lamented that the death wasn't a very good one—the character should have bled longer.[27]

The military uses killing simulators such as Doom to desensitize soldiers to killing. The military learned that it is one thing to train soldiers in marksmanship, but another to get them to actually kill another human being, and these simulators are successful at getting them to kill. In World War II, when soldiers trained using bull's-eye targets, in combat they fired at the enemy between 10 and 15 percent of the time. In Vietnam, when soldiers trained with silhouettes shaped like men, the firing rate increased to 95 percent. The use of a human-like target effectively desensitized them to the killing.[28]

Gender Roles and Sex

A study published in 2001 found that only 17 percent of the characters in games were female and even fewer than that were characters controlled by a player. The very few female protagonists wear skimpy, tight costumes, even as they engage in hand-to-hand combat. The study also reported that 21 percent of the female characters had bare breasts, 7 percent of them fully exposed, and 13 percent had bare buttocks, with 8 percent of them fully bare.[29] While the list of games studied does include the "M" rated Tomb Raider, it did not include the much more sexually explicit Duke Nukem, Grand Theft Auto III, Grand Theft: Vice City, Doom or BMX XXX. If the study were repeated now, the rates of nudity and degrading portrayals would undoubtedly be much higher.

Most of the female characters that do exist in games appear hypersexualized featuring enormous breasts and very small waists.[30] Lara Croft in Tomb Raider is such a character, and, in fact, players have the ability to strip her so she appears naked. In "M" rated games, female characters are often prostitutes and strippers.[31] The extreme sport biking game, BMX XXX, features topless female bikers and video clips of live nude strippers. In addition, in this game, players can create female characters and control their breast size.[32] These images of women concern game critics. The National Institute on Media and the Family finds images of nudes and semi-nudes—not only sexist but demeaning. Further, the sexist portrayals reinforce attitudes that women are simply sex objects and teach boys to disrespect women.[33] These portrayals negatively affect girls who learn that these sexist and nude images are what they should aspire to, while boys learn how to treat girls from these images.[34]

Racial Representations

A study of video games conducted between January and May 2001 found a lack of racial diversity among the characters in the games. Over half of the characters in the games were White, and nearly every hero was a White male. While 22 percent of the characters were African-American, they played stereotypical sports figures.[35] The games Ready 2 Rumble and NBA Street feature Black males with huge Afros, great rap skills and Ebonic speech patterns.[36] In Final Fantasy VII, the only Black character, Barett, cursed and used Ebonic speech patterns.[37] In NFL2K, the Black running backs "prance and dance" in the end zone, and in Ready 2 Rumble the Black boxer, Afro Thunder, gives a James Brown scream while entering the ring.[38] Even Jet Grind Radio, a game set in the Black hip-hop culture, features very few Black characters.[39] Because of advances in technology, game designers give characters authentic and identifiable racial characteristics. Game designer, Guy Miller, creator of Shadow Man, explained that they used an African-American for the voice of Shadow Man and digitally captured a Black boxer's walk to give him a catlike stride. This very authenticity is controversial, with some critics claiming that it creates further racial stereotyping with what one critic called "high-tech blackface."[40]

The 2001 study featured no Latina, and very few Latino characters. The Latino characters usually played sports figures[41] such as the wild Mexican boxer, Angel (Raging) Rivera in Ready 2 Rumble.[42]

Only three Native American characters appeared in the games in the 2001 study. Gamers controlled only one character, a wrestler; the others were simply props controlled by the computer, not the gamer.[43]

The rare Asian/Pacific Islanders usually appeared as props. The player controlled characters usually appeared as sports figures, often wrestlers or fighters.[44] In Ready 2 Rumble, Salua Tua, a former Sumo wrestler, appears as a Hawaiian heavy-weight boxer.[45]

The Industry Defense

In advertising the sex-loaded game BMX XXX, Acclaim Entertainment promised to "Keep it Dirty." In spite of this suggestive promise, in response to criticism of the explicit nature of the sexuality, the chief executive of Acclaim, Greg Fischbach, claims the game is simply "humorous."[46] A spokesman for the very violent Doom, argues that his company simply created something entertaining. He put the game on a par with the cartoons, Wile E. Coyote and *Road Runner*.[47]

Another member of the gaming industry tried to deflect criticism claiming that the games, at $50 each, are too expensive for kids to afford. However, a report released in 2000 found that the average teen boy spends $70 per week on himself; the average girl, $64.[48] With that kind of money, the price is not likely to prohibit kids from getting the games.

Also, the head of the International Digital Software Association, Doug Lowenstein, claims that there is "absolutely no evidence, none" that video game playing causes aggressive behavior.[49] However, while the research is meager, the study mentioned earlier about the effects of violent game playing, not only found a relationship between playing and increased aggression, but also concluded that the interactive nature of the games makes playing them even more likely to cause aggression than watching television violence — and thousands of studies link television violence to aggressive behavior.[50]

In a telling comment, a programmer at Raven Software, Mike Gummelt, admitted that "we'd have to be either extremely stubborn, in deep denial, or lying to say that the violence in our games doesn't affect people."[51]

Conclusions

This analysis of the current selection of video games presents some serious problems for today's children. Kids easily get hold of games with an "M" rating, filled with graphic violence and sex. The games abuse women, giving problematic messages to both boys and girls who may become desensitized to the violence and think this behavior is acceptable. In addition to negative gender stereotypes, when games feature ethnic minorities they are often stereotypical and negative. These games contain powerful negative messages.

—What You Can Do—

- Be involved with your children when they are selecting video games. Pay attention to the ESRB ratings for the games.

- Rent a game before you buy it.

- Observe your children as they are playing a game. Some games take up to 100 hours to finish. Most parents can't spend that amount of time with a game, but many games get much more graphic toward the end of the game compared to the beginning. So try to catch a snippet of what is happening well into the game.

- Set priorities. For example, homework needs to be complete before playing video games.

- Set limits on how much time per day your child may play.

- Look for two-player games that encourage cooperation between the players.

- If you notice an increase in aggressive behavior in your children after they have played video games, set strict limits on how much and what kind of games they can play.

- Analyze the portrayal of gender and racial stereotypes with your children. Discuss what stereotypes are and why they may be harmful.

Chapter 9

Porn and Pedophilia:

Stops on the Information Superhighway

A 15-year-old girl encountered Larry Stackhouse, a 43-year-old man whom she met in an Internet chat room. The conversations became progressively more intimate and sexual, and after a month Stackhouse arranged to pick up the girl and her friend for a face-to-face meeting. He traveled over 800 miles from Philadelphia to Alabama to pick up the girls. The girls thought it would be an adventure, but Stackhouse drove them to Philadelphia where he sexually assaulted the girl for three days—until her friend got to a phone and got help from their parents.[1]

What happened to the Internet that Al Gore raved about in the 1997 Internet/Online Summit? Gore talked about the Internet as an essential tool and a glorious opportunity to improve kids' learning. He also claimed that the Internet would allow our "civilization to take a quantum leap forward" and change the way we relate to the huge amounts of information available to us.[2] It certainly has changed how we relate to information, but the leaps have not always been forward ones.

Child Pornography

By the 1980s, the crackdown on child pornography in the United States had been so effective that law enforcement officials believed it was eliminated. In those days traffickers in child pornography had to use the mail and get photos developed at a public place, so they could easily be caught. With the development of the Internet, lurid child pornography thrives because pictures from digital cameras needn't be professionally developed. Furthermore, the anonymity of the Internet makes the dissemination of pornography difficult to catch.

Child pornography rings exist world-wide. When officials broke up the international Wonderland Club they found three quarters of a million child porn images in Great Britain alone and millions more around the globe. Prospective members of the Wonderland Club had to provide 10,000 images of child pornography to join. The images that officials found included infants as young as three months old involved in explicit sex acts.[3] In 2000, American officials cracked the Orchid Club in the United States and found over 750,000 images of child pornography. Some of the children were only 18 months old. The speed of the Internet means that images multiply quickly and world-wide. A single image can be multiplied to several thousand in just 24 hours.[4]

Pedophilia

People with similar interests send and read messages in online sites called chat rooms. A kid can go to a chat room, type in a nickname for him or herself, and then participate in chatting. Some chat rooms have rules, and a moderator screens all messages before they are posted. However, members can write just about anything in unmoderated chat rooms.

Some kids purposely go to chat rooms they find titillating and dangerous. They intentionally flirt and verbally play at seducing people they think are creepy and perverted.[5] Teen and pre-teen girls post nude or semi-nude pictures of themselves online, some of them featuring sexual behavior, in hopes of getting gifts from other surfers.[6] Chat room members often sexually harass girls, who are at a loss as to what to do when they are asked their bra size or are sent photos of nude men.[7]

Pedophiles, those who fantasize about or actually engage in sex with children, also frequent chat rooms. Posing as kids themselves, they form close "friendships" with kids online. They typically sit back and observe the chat room conversation, looking for a promising victim. Pedophiles no longer need to lurk near a schoolyard or park playground to scope out a likely target. They begin conversing about innocent topics such as what kind of music the kid likes and complimenting the kid on how nice he or she seems.

Once a relationship has begun, the pedophile asks the kid to chat in a private chat room for one-on-one conversations. Then he or she starts "grooming" the target. He or she asks for more personal information, such as, "What's your family like," and "Can you use the computer in private?" The pedophile tells the kid to make sure this friendship is "our little secret." Then the level of intimacy escalates into questions about the kid's sexuality, expressions of love for the kid and concerns about whether the kid trusts the pedophile. The conversation primarily becomes one about risk assessment—how likely the kid is to fall for the sincerity of the relationship.[8]

This grooming process may take months, and once the pedophile feels trusted, he exposes the child to pornography. This encourages the victim to think that these sexual behaviors are okay and helps to prepare and even entice the child to participate in sex.[9] Then the pedophile may arrange for a real world meeting, kept secret from family, of course. Indeed, 25 percent of kids using chat rooms have been asked for face-to-face meetings, and one in 10 have done it. This "cyber stalking" can lead to abduction or molestation of the child.[10]

Investigators in Minnesota uncovered another ingenious method of identifying possible targets for pedophiles. In the 1990s, the prison at Lino Lakes, just north of Minneapolis, ran a telemarketing business to help inmates earn money for college tuition upon their release. One convicted pedophile used the computer to identify possible victims. He had access to many local newspapers from small towns all over the state through the prison library. He compiled a huge database (of mostly girls three to 12 years old) from features about kids in these papers—birthday greetings, school activities and contestants for "Little Miss" beauty pageants, for example. He provided comments about each kid, such as "latchkey kid," "chubby," "takes piano lessons," and included the town in which they lived with map coordinates to their locations. Although not yet confirmed, authorities fear that the list was for sale to pedophiles not in prison.[11]

Internet pedophilia carries with it some extraordinary, offensive wrinkles. One is that it allows a video camera to connect to the Internet, broadcasting the assault in real time. Members of the Orchid Club not only viewed the abuse of a five-year-old in real time, but sent requests to the abuser detailing what acts they wanted to see. Officials also uncovered videos of the assault of a 9- or 10-year-old girl that included bondage.[12]

The home page of a couple in Texas included nasty links to sites called "Child Rape" and "Children Forced to Porn." They also posted ads from parents offering to swap their children for sex with other parents.[13] Even more horrible, officials found two pedophiles in Virginia posting to a computer bulletin board to find a boy to use in a "snuff" film. When they were discovered, police found that they had a large supply of muriatic acid to use to destroy the boy's corpse.[14]

One police unit in Virginia aggressively pursues these predators. Members of Operation Blue Ridge Thunder pose as youngsters in chat rooms to track and catch these predators. One tracker, Jamie Watson, posed as a 13-year-old girl and met "Dr. Evil" in a chat room. They arranged to meet, and, in what the trackers described as the worst case they had seen, they found evidence suggesting that Dr. Evil planned to murder the girl. They found an ax handle and a knife in his car. Jamie also posed as a 13-year-old girl to chat with Timothy Farnum, a 45-year-old school bus driver from Albany, New York. When Farnum sent the "girl" a one-way airline ticket to Albany, the police officers were there to successfully catch him as he met the plane. While these are but two examples of success, the Operation Blue Ridge team notes that there are thousands of adults looking to assault kids on the Internet every day.[15]

Internet Pornography

Internet porn, also called the online adult industry, reaps $1.1 billion annually, and 72 million people visit those sites each year. Because adult pornography is legal, children easily find it. An enormous amount of both soft and hardcore porn exists; it includes sites where viewers watch live performers and can request certain sexual activities.[16] To keep children away from such pornography is difficult, and information on the impact of seeing it is limited.[17] However, there is evidence that exposure to porn before age 14 is related to increased likelihood that the viewer will commit a sexual assault, such as rape. In addition, more than three-fourths of child molesters report using pornography to stimulate them to commit sexual assault. They also use pornography to show children what they want the child to do and to reduce a child's reluctance to participate in the act. Researchers also believe that viewing pornography, in which no negative consequences occur, is related to the increased incidence of sexually transmitted diseases. Alarmingly, in the U.S., one of every four kids who engage in sex contract a sexually transmitted disease each year, resulting in three million cases of STD annually. Currently, twice as many teenagers contract syphilis each year compared to the mid-1980s.[18]

Internet access in public libraries presents the problem of kids visiting pornographic sites. A woman in New Jersey watched a young boy locate pornography on the Internet in a library. She described the boy, who appeared to be about 12, as riveted to the screen. A mother in Washington found her three- and six-year-old sons watching a man and a woman have oral sex online by looking at a computer screen in the children's section of the library.[19]

A Minneapolis librarian complained that a group of men would spend 10 hours a day surfing for porn, often intentionally sitting within eyeshot of kids.[20] David Burt, a librarian who conducted a survey of libraries concerning Internet pornography in public libraries, claimed that librarians witnessed adults trading in child pornography, teaching kids how to find pornography and masturbating at computer terminals.[21]

These incidents and many others like it prompted Congress to pass the Children's Internet Protection Act (CIPA) in December 2001. The law requires libraries that receive certain federal funds to install filters on their computers. Not long after, the American Library Association, along with the ACLU, filed suits claiming that the law violated free-speech rights and discriminated against anyone without access to a home computer. They also pointed out that filters may prevent people from accessing sites about health issues (e.g., prostate cancer),[22] and at the same time encourage kids to get to porn "stealth" sites having innocuous names like "Barbie," "Disney" and "ESPN."[23] Inspite of these flaws in filtering, in June 2003, the Supreme Court narrowly upheld the law.[24]

Some public libraries have refused to filter and choose instead to absorb the loss of the federal funds. The Berkeley Public Library claimed that they were doing the right and principled thing to refuse to filter because the filters limit access to such useful sites as those offering information about AIDS and breast cancer. Furthermore, the chair of the library board noted that his nine-year-old son couldn't access a site about "cats" because the word had sexual connotations and the filter would also block the Bush-Cheney site because of the words "Bush" and "Dick." That library's $10 million budget, mostly provided by local funding, will not hurt from the loss of federal funds. But other libraries can't afford the loss of federal funding.[25] Those libraries must restrict their patrons' access to many valuable sites.

Chat Rooms and Cyber Stalking

Chat rooms often focus on entertainment, such as the room for the rock group, Limp Bizkit. Many kids enjoyed the chat room. So did 20-year-old Christian Hunold, who used several aliases to gain information about the kids who gathered there. Soon, he knew what the kids were wearing, what they did on Friday nights and who was mad at whom. Then he escalated to directing kids to pornographic sites, and creating "hit" lists of students and teachers. Although kids found the messages, as well as his alias (a boast about raping girls) disgusting and perverted, they continued to communicate with him. In all, Hunold chatted with 40 eighth graders in one Massachusetts middle school. At the end of the school year, a police officer brought the school principal a web page that included a picture of the school in the crosshairs of a rifle, and also a picture of the principal with blood pouring from his head and chest.[26]

In the fall of 2003, "Dear Abby" printed several letters from distraught parents who described their daughters' experiences with pedophiles they met on the Internet. One mother told of her 13-year-old daughter who met up with a man who claimed to be 15 in a chat room. The man turned out to be 37 years old and had previously molested a 10-year-old girl. Another described how her 16-year-old stepdaughter became involved with an Internet pedophile who claimed to be 17 but was actually 56 years old.[27] A third mother wrote about her daughter who at 10 was pursued online by a 17-year-old boy who was a suicidal mental patient. When the daughter tried to end the relationship, he threatened to kill her and her family, then commit suicide. It took her family over a year to end the relationship, get him in a mental facility and get a restraining order to prevent him from contacting the daughter.[28]

Instant Messaging, Websites and Cyber Bullying

Instant Messaging (IM) allows kids to communicate in real time with people online. When kids get an IM account, they fill out a profile that includes personal information. This profile becomes part of an Internet directory available to anyone. Kids then create "buddy lists" of people with whom they want to communicate. Many teens say that this is the main way they communicate with their friends and 74 percent of teens admit to use of IM.[29] Because kids use pseudonyms, they can communicate with relative anonymity. This has some benefits—shy kids can become more confident on-screen.

But problems occur when kids share or steal each other's passwords and then anonymously bully other kids. Some of them create multiple IM identities and use the secret one to bully. Fifty-six percent of teens who use IM or email have more than one account and 37 percent of kids say they have used IM to say something they would not say face-to-face.[30] A teen near Boston used IM to send violent and sexually threatening messages to several girls; a restraining order was placed on him to prevent him from contacting the girls using IM or email.[31] Kids can send abusive messages, sign off and, if confronted in person, claim they know nothing about it. Schools usually do nothing about it, claiming the abuse happened off school property. Parents of bullies do nothing, claiming the child has First Amendment rights. Previously a victim could get home to escape the bullying, but with IM, kids are vulnerable 24 hours a day.[32]

The presence of your kid's profile in an Internet directory presents the risk that strangers can IM with your child and infiltrate his or her "buddy list."[33] Instant Message spamming is another way imposters make their way onto IMers' buddy lists. Nicole Fann was at work on her computer when an IM appeared asking her to check out the website for "hot girl." She was suspicious enough to block the sender from her IM account.[34] But kids may innocently add dangerous people to their IM lists.

In addition to the risks of chat rooms and Instant Messaging, kids also create hateful websites about other kids to bully them. One day a high school student in Ontario got an email message from a fellow student urging him to check out a certain website. He did and found his photo and the name of the site the same as his name. The site was full of nasty comments about him and his family. He was accused of pedophilia, raping little boys using the date rape drug and other sexually repulsive things. The site ruined his reputation. Furthermore, millions of people saw the accusations. He began isolating himself from other students and hurt so badly that he finished his final year of school at home.[35]

Newsgroups

Thousands of newsgroups exist online where people can post messages on topics ranging from recipes, ideas, news, business and just about anything you can think of. Each newsgroup posts messages that pertain to the subject of the newsgroup. Once you join a newsgroup, you may post messages. If others respond to your message, a "thread" has been created. When people stop responding to a message, the thread dies. In a moderated newsgroup, someone sorts through the messages that are sent and posts only those that pertain to the group's subject. However, most newsgroups lack moderators, and members can post any message.

Even pedophiles form news groups. An Internet newsgroup called alt.support.boy-lovers offers encouragement and a sense of validation to pedophiles. Pedophiles frequently use the groups to bolster their self-concepts.[36]

Some Internet newsgroups appear to be useful and appropriate for kids. A search of several newsgroups turned up one called <alt.school.homework-help> that assists kids with homework. Another, <k12.chat.junior> included threads about kids' problems with math. A site called <school.pupils>, described as discussion and chat between pupils, noted that it currently has no messages. Others with promising names included <k12.chat.elementary>, and <alt.speech.debate>, but they clearly targeted teachers. A series of links under the major link, <the linq.high> sounded promising, but Yahoo said they could not be found. So it appears that there are not many active Internet newsgroups designed for kids. Most groups are for adults, and kids should use them with great caution.

Indeed, some newsgroups exist to distribute pornographic images. The Child Protection Society's website described newsgroups that featured pictures ranging from grown men sodomizing young boys to the rape of an infant girl.[37]

The prefix "alt." stands for alternate newsgroups, meaning they exist because no current newsgroup is covering that topic. A mythology exists that the prefix "alt." stands for "alternative lifestyle," but this isn't necessarily true.

Internet Gambling

Kids' gambling often begins innocently enough as parents let their little ones scratch lottery tickets to see if they've won. Many families visiting Las Vegas stay at Circus Circus, a casino hotel that features a Jungle Jamboree for kids where they play casino games designed for kids. With the advent of online gambling, gambling among young people has grown into a huge problem. In Montreal, at age 16, Adam and his friends began an Internet betting pool to accompany their avid interest in professional hockey. Researchers at McGill University in Montreal worry that online gambling has become too easy for kids to access. The off-shore sites have no regulation about who can play, and once a kid has a parent's credit card, he or she can gamble freely.[38] Although in the U.S. and Canada it's illegal to run an Internet gambling website, over 2,000 foreign-based, off-shore sites offer children and others access to online betting.[39]

The American Psychiatric Association, concerned with the online gambling problems of high school and college students, issued an advisory about it stating that virtually every study of problematic gambling has concluded that high school- and college-aged kids have the most severe problems with gambling. The advisory concluded that the high problem rate in kids can at least partially be attributed to how easy it is to gamble on the Internet. In addition, the APA cited the lack of restrictions on the age one can play, the times during which gambling takes place and the types of games kids play as factors contributing to the problem. They also note that many online game sites that aren't gambling sites have links to gambling sites to lure potential gamblers. Additionally, some sites offer discounts and free gifts to get kids started.[40]

The sums of money young people lose on Internet gambling can be staggering. Kids sometimes lose tens of thousands of dollars. One kid lost $70,000 he had been stealing from his family. Another gambled his college tuition money away. His father paid for another tuition bill, but the kid quit school, got a refund and lost that too.[41] Another student lost $10,000 in three months betting on sports. College students have access to virtual casinos on their dorm room computers, and all they need is a credit card number to play. Eighty percent of college kids have one credit card, and a third of them have four or more cards. The director of Addiction Studies at Harvard, Dr. Howard Shaffer, says the draw is so great that it rivals addiction to crack cocaine, especially for young people.[42]

The Internet and Education

A middle school student from a small town praised the Internet because her school's science books are very old, and she boasted that she can get reams of up-to-date material online. Another girl described it as "your local library times a thousand." Students use chat rooms for study sessions before tests and to discuss material with students all over the country. They also use it to research prospective colleges and career choices.[43]

Students also admit to some unethical uses of the Internet. One student explained that he could find all of the answers online to questions in specific workbooks in which he had assignments. He also confessed that he finds essays on the Internet that match something he's been assigned to write. He said that he doesn't "totally plagiarize" these essays —he merely "changes some of the words," but uses the overall ideas.[44] Many websites even offer term papers, book reports and research papers to students. PaperCamp.com provides papers written by various talented students for free. In return, the site asks a student to donate a paper he or she has written. TermPaper.net has over 20,000 ghost-written papers on file, and they are ready for instant downloading at prices as low as $4 per page. DueNow.com will provide a "custom-written" paper in one day for $32 per page. It warns that students should not use free online paper databases because teachers now use anti-plagiarism databases to ensure that a paper is original. DueNow.com claims that their papers are copyrighted and aren't available to the anti-plagiarism databases; therefore, they are worth the high price.

Hate Groups

Before the Internet, hate groups such as neo-Nazi, White supremacist, anti-gay and religious hate groups recruited using post office boxes, "plain brown wrappers" and rallies in out-of-the way places.[45] Since the Internet, hate groups reach millions of people they couldn't before. Many of them actively recruit kids as young as nine years old. Between 1995 and 1999 the number of online hate groups grew from just one to over 2,000. [46] Stormfront is a White supremacist site created by Don Black, who took over as leader of the Ku Klux Klan in 1980. In 2001, 3,315 people had registered as Stormfront members.[47] The site also features Stormfront for Kids, also a White supremacist site whose webmaster claims to be 14 years old. He explains that he left public school because so many White minds are wasted — slow kids get attention, while political correctness diminishes the achievements of Whites.

The White supremacist group, World Church of the Creator, also has a large presence on the Internet. It gives kids a sense of purpose and excitement, and it appeals to young adolescent males who find hatred exhilarating. Further, the sites that specialize in attracting nine-year-olds give the kids a sense of belonging that may not be coming from their parents or school.[48] The World Church of the Creator site includes a coloring book for kids as well as a crossword puzzle that asks kids for the word that starts with the letter "N" that is "a crude reference to blacks." The appeal to kids is reinforced with a special page created by someone claiming to be a 10-year-old named Derek.

Posse Comitatus, another White supremacist group, features an image of a lynching and the words, "It's time for old-fashioned American justice." It also appeals to kids with an advice column supposedly written by a 14-year-old named Jeff.[49]

Holocaust revisionist groups maintain that the concentration camps never existed. Hundreds of Ku Klux Klan groups exist, and the group, "Wake up or Die," devotes itself to unmasking and dismantling the "parasitic monsters who feed on White 'Gentile' Americans." One writer noted that hate groups and gangs both attract the lonely and isolated by giving kids the feeling of acceptance, as if they're part of a family.[50]

—What You Can Do—

- Watch for warning signs that your children might be using the Internet to look at pornography:

  Minimizing the screen when you come into the room

  Spending lots of time online

  Erasing the history file on the computer

  Getting lower grades than usual

- Get a filtering system for Internet site access. *PC Magazine* reviews those devices. Some of them allow you to program the sites you want access to. Others are pre-programmed. Net Nanny and Cybersitter are just two of many that are available. Also, check out www.FilterReview.com for reviews of filters.

- Place your computer in a public space in your house.

- Check the history of the sites your children visit. Pornographic sites are not the only dangerous sites. Gambling and hate group sites are also problems. Do this:

  > In a Windows system, go to Start>Search>Files, then type in the word "cache."

  > For Macintosh, go to File>Find> then look for the word "cache."

- In chat rooms, be sure your children do not use their real names and that the selected name doesn't indicate whether your children are male or female.

- Tell your children never to agree to meet someone they've met online in person unless you are with them.

- Know your children's screen names.

- Children under age eight should not use chat rooms at all.

- Older kids should visit only moderated chat rooms.

- Teach them never to leave the public area of a chat room and go into a private room.

- Tell your children never to respond to harassing or hateful messages.

- Tell your children not to fill out profiles. If they must, advise them to give as little information as possible.

- Tell your children never to give out personal information.

- Tell your children to give their passwords to no one but you.

- Remind them that people online may or may not be who they really are.

- Never allow a photo of you or your children online.

- If your children receive unwanted sexual or threatening messages, do not hesitate to go to the police with the information.

- Find out whether or not the library your children frequent uses a filtering system on its computers. If it doesn't, warn them to use extra caution, and do so yourself, when your children use the Internet at the library.

- If your children use the Internet to do research for school, remind them that any nut can post something online and that there are no "net police" checking for the accuracy of the information.

- Explain to them that using someone else's work as your own is plagiarism and that it carries such serious penalties as automatic failure of a course to being expelled from school.

- Warn your children about the addictive nature of gambling. Do not give them your credit card numbers. If you have already done it, seriously consider closing that account and getting another one.

Chapter 10

Taming the Beast:

Becoming Media Literate

Marsha Smith, a teacher in Roseville, Minnesota, video-
tapes the Super Bowl broadcasts and brings the tapes to her
class so that she and her students can analyze the commercials. They discuss the way advertisers sell products, using
not just product features, but also emotional appeals gen-
erated by the commercials. Her students note, for example,
that a particular Tylenol ad doesn't really sell the drug's
ability to kill pain, but rather the emotional pleasure a
father and son get from tossing around a football.[1]

Consider how many hours your children spend in their
free time reading poetry, short stories and novels. Then
think about how much time they spend in school analyzing
that literature and maybe even writing it—perhaps several
hours a week. But what about the hours your children spend
watching TV? How much do they know about how to analyze
those mass mediated messages?

The average child watches television for 23 to 28 hours
a week; but few, if any, know how to study it. Kids need to
consume media intelligently so they aren't unduly influenced by what they hear and see. Experts who study this

process of learning to analyze how the media works. Call it the development of "media literacy."

Sideshow Bob Gets You into the Tent

During the nineteenth and much of the twentieth centuries, the midways at state and county fairs featured sideshows. The shows took place in tents with featured acts such as the Wild Man of Borneo, the Bearded Woman, the Fire Eater, the Sword Swallower, Hitler's Car, Crab Boy, Siamese Twins and Midget Boxers. A pitchman stood outside the tent to hype the show and lure people into the tent, teasing them with peeks at the attractions in the tent that could be seen fully for the price of admission.

In much the same way, the media serve as "pitchmen," delivering audiences to sponsors. Media are not in business to deliver programming to viewers, but rather to get audiences to buy products. *NFL Football* delivers male audiences to marketers of beer and cars. *All My Children* sells women viewers on detergents and feminine products. *Hey Arnold!* conveys kids to tasty treats and water guns.

Cosmopolitan magazine hands over women to cosmetics, perfume and shampoo companies. *Maxim* delivers young men to athletic shoes and new cars, and *Seventeen* brings teenage girls to facial cleansers and acne medication.

The time-honored *Chicago Tribune* delivers readers to high-end department stores, up-scale supermarkets, and various restaurants and cultural events.

Television programming and print advertising get viewers and readers into the "tent," so they can see the real "show." Many people don't realize that this is the true purpose of the media.

Nothing is Left to Chance

Ask anyone what the best brand of turkey is and research shows they are likely to answer, "Butterball." At Thanksgiving time, those Butterball turkeys always look better than anything that comes out of the average cook's oven. No wonder.

People called "food stylists" are frequently called in to "dress" a food product. It is reported that to make a hamburger from McDonald's or Burger King look perfect takes a "food stylist" approximately 10 steps, using only the most perfect buns and gluing extra sesame seeds on them, if necessary.[2]

Even "reality" shows like *Survivor* and *Temptation Island* don't show everything. Editors modify these shows for various reasons. For example, *Survivor* broadcasted footage of a participant who had been badly burned in the Australian outback. When *Survivor* got severe criticism for the image, the producer pointed out that in reality the images were much more disgusting. Editors had removed the most grisly footage. In another episode, editors removed distasteful footage of a participant urinating on the arm of another person to relieve the pain of sea urchin bites.[3]

Most media illiterate viewers assume that talk shows like *Late Night with David Letterman* are spontaneous and live, but they are not. Actual taping for late night viewing occurs during the late afternoon or early evening, and producers remove offensive guests, their comments and/or portions of the show if they happen to run overtime.

Documentaries (which encourage viewers to believe they are objective) always have been heavily and intentionally edited. Producers want to transmit a specific, persuasive message (e.g., that a conspiracy was involved in the Kennedy assassination), and that message depends on the footage that gets to the final program. Programs like *National Geographic* specials about nature encourage viewers to believe that the behaviors they see (e.g., combative behavior or mating rituals) are readily observable. In reality, crews of camerapersons might spend days or weeks in the field to capture the precise footage that creates the desired effect. *National Geographic* also buys hours of footage from "stock" footage companies, freelancers and museums from all around the world.

Additionally, documentaries are accompanied by music that adds to the narration and the effect of the program. Meanwhile, producers know that viewers find black-and-white documentaries especially realistic and believable. They may intentionally use black-and-white footage to add to the persuasive effect of the documentary. The resulting "documentary" becomes a "virtual" documentary.

Most viewers (including children) also assume that news programs are objective and never biased. That isn't the case either. Watch and compare FOX News Channel with CNN and CBS News on the same day. You'll discover considerable differences, reflecting how editors and producers develop stories to be aired from hundreds of hours of footage. For example, Fox News tends to use more sensational images than either CNN or CBS News. FOX News Channel stories might focus on blood and guts, grieving survivors, and the tawdry details of Michael Jackson's indictment for child molestation. It also tends to feature a right-wing political bias. On the other hand CNN or CBS News is more likely to focus on in-depth analysis, featuring experts who interpret the evidence behind the accident or the crime.

A Minnesota teacher of media literacy was alarmed that his high school students erroneously thought *Hard Copy* and *Inside Edition* presented "the news." He was dismayed to learn that these students used the tabloid shows as their main news source.[4] In fact, these shows have much more in common with the *National Enquirer* than *The Washington Post*. Viewers who believe that television tabloids give a realistic picture of what is going on and what is important in the world are misled and have a remarkably distorted view of the world.

Media ownership also affects news and programming. Al Franken, in his book, *Lies (and the Lying Liars Who Tell Them)*, reports that Rupert Murdoch's News Corporation owns FOX Broadcasting Company and *TV Guide*, and their agenda is to promote rightwing causes as well as the financial aims of Murdoch.[5] In addition, General Electric owns NBC, MSNBC, Bravo, the Sci-Fi Channel and USA Network. General Electric also owns the media conglomerate Vivendi, one of the two largest private water companies in the world, operating in over 90 countries. This ownership might well affect a producer's choices about how to cover the growth of private water companies, energy issues, pollution problems and the price fixing of electricity. Another example is The Walt Disney Company; Disney owns ABC, ABC Family Channel, Disney Channel, ESPN, The History Channel, Lifetime, Toon Disney, Touchstone Pictures, Miramax Films and many other media companies, as well as the Mighty Ducks of Anaheim, part of the Anaheim Angels, and many theme parks. This near monopoly of the media influences the fall line-up of programs and films broadcast on ABC and likely slants news coverage of The Disney Company's activities in a positive light. In all likelihood it even affects coverage of political news. For instance, Time Warner Cable, Viacom and Disney own nearly two-thirds of all TV channels.[6] Just think of the implications of this ownership on the content of what they broadcast.

Analyzing Commercial Messages in Magazine Ads*

Once the sideshow barker has convinced you to come into the "tent," the attractions (i.e., commercial messages) you see have been expertly constructed, even faked, as was the Butterball turkey, by the "food stylists." Advertisers sell products and brands, but they sell much more. These carefully created commercials sell emotions, values and beliefs, as well as the brand they promote, and they try to involve the reader/viewer in the construction of the meaning of the commercial message. This audience participation enhances the impact of the ad. Ads also reinforce the values of society, telling readers who and what are important. They show that society values conspicuous consumption, for example, and that White men remain the most important people in our society.

Few people realize that various production techniques carry specific connotations that help create the meaning of an ad. For example, bright lighting suggests fun and happiness, while muted lighting suggests romance or a somber mood. A low camera angle shot, in which the camera is placed physically lower than the subject of the shot, gives the subject power and dominance. On the other hand, a high angle shot, in which the camera shoots down on the subject, makes the subject look weak or subordinate. These simple techniques are often used in political ads and news coverage as well as product ads. A canted angle shot, in which the cameraperson uses a handheld camera tilted at an angle, skewing the horizon, gives dynamism and energy to a shot. It can make a dull product or candidate look exciting and attractive. A close-up shot indicates that a person or thing is very important, or that the shot portrays intimacy. Close-ups of stars or politicians encourage readers to think they really know the person in the ad.

A Curve ad in *Glamour* (Aug. 2002, p. 77) shows five adults playing pool together. Pictured are three women and two men. One woman is clearly White (straight blond hair, fair skin), another probably White (dark, straight hair, light

---

* The analyses that follow can be generalized and applied to any magazine ad. While those analyzed here do apply to specific ads, I was unable to get permission to reprint the ads. Consequently, I have described the ad in some detail, and included the citation (magazine title, date and page number) for readers who may want to seek out the original ad.

skin), one may be Black (somewhat kinky, curly hair, medium skin tone), and all are dressed in upscale fashions. Of the two men, one is White in an open-collared sports shirt, the other appears Asian and is wearing a monogrammed shirt, perhaps a bowling shirt or that of a gas station attendant. All of the people are smiling and laughing, and they are within what is called "intimate distance" of each other. In this ad, the camera shoots the people straight on in an objective shot, connoting neither power nor weakness of the subjects. In addition, the ad tells readers that society values racial harmony by showing people in the ad ranging from the very blonde, fair woman on the right to the darker woman on the left. Further, the ad indicates that society values class harmony. Notice that the well-dressed and upscale women enjoy playing pool in a bar with a blue-collar man, suggested by his monogrammed shirt. The presence of three women and two men suggests that this is a group of friends, rather than a dating situation, placing value on mixed gender friendships. The ad encourages readers to become involved in the ad, asking the reader to finish the thought, i. e., that using Curve may make for an exciting adventure. In addition the word "Curve" in the large letters and the presence of 10 Curve products in the ad encourage brand recognition. The ad also uses the most powerful word in advertising, "free," and protects their offer with the disclaimer, "while supplies last," creating a sense of urgency. The ad actually tells readers nothing about the brand features, but rather ties the ad to emotions and values.

Next, I've examined an ad for Musk by alyssa ashley, which ran in *Cosmopolitan* magazine (Aug., 2002, p. 41). The elements in this ad create an entirely different mood from the ad for Curves. The sepia tone of the ad and the muted lighting give this ad a romantic flavor. The low angle of the camera (i.e., the camera is lower than eye level of the subjects) makes the people the most important element in the ad, and most readers would infer that the state of undress of the couple implies that the effect left by Musk will be sexual. The woman's broad smile suggests happiness and pleasure. The copy delivers the message that wearing Musk will get you sex, happiness and a long-term relationship. This ad also capitalizes on emotions and values rather than the actual brand.

The ad for Pantene from *Ebony* (Jan., 2004, p, 17) and other ads targeted at women of color feature other emotions and values. Many ads include bright lighting that creates a pleasant, upbeat mood with low angle shots of the models, thus making them the central focus of the ad. However, in terms of values, virtually all of the models have straight hair and relatively light skin. These features tell women of color that society devalues their dark skin and natural hair. Since straightening black hair damages it terribly, a large market exists for the various conditioners and moisturizers Pantene sells. This ad does sell the product features of being able to condition dry hair. But it also sells the value of straight hair and light skin.

The ad for diamonds that appeared in *People* (Nov. 17, 2003, p. 15) shows a black backdrop with two diamond rings —one big, the other extremely big. The ad blatantly values conspicuous consumption. The copy encourages readers to select a ring of one-half carat—or more. The stark contrast of the rings on the black foil background that jewelers use to display diamonds highlights the importance of the diamonds. There are no distractions from the importance of the size of the diamonds, not even people. The selling points are the size of the diamond and the value that "bigger is better."

The ad for the Sony Handycam, from *Men's Health* (Feb. 2004, p. 13) features riders on a roller coaster, taking a picture using the Handycam. The Handycam is shot straight on and in full focus, differentiating it from the blurred roller coaster. The camera angle on the Handycam leaves the people in the roller coaster below the lens level of the camera, making the Handycam more important than the people. The fact

that all of the people on the ride are Caucasian suggests that
the target audience for the ad is White people. The speed
of the roller coaster, indicated by the blur in the shot, plus
the bright lighting, and the terrified image of the man in the
viewfinder, combine to sell excitement—the ability to watch
your life pass in front of you over and over. The ad does
describe product features, but in a font so small that the words
are overpowered by the excitement of the image. The ad urges
readers to connect a Handycam with excitement.

Next let's consider an ad for the Toyota RAV4 from *People*
magazine (Dec. 1, 2003, p. 77) which also features speed and
power with the background of the shot blurred, as if the car
is speeding. There is a canted angle to this camera shot, the
horizon is skewed; this contributes to a feeling of energy and
dynamism. In addition, the RAV4 is driving up and away.
The bright lighting tells readers that driving a RAV4 creates
pleasure and enjoyment. Furthermore, the copy tells readers
that driving the RAV4 will give you energy, thus emphasizing the stimulating boost RAV4s give to driving. The ad tells
readers that society values power and speed, and the relatively small images of people at the bottom of the page
reinforce the importance of the car compared to the people.

An ad for Skyy, a citrus flavored vodka, that ran in
Cosmopolitan (Aug., 2002, p. 131) is of interest. It sells sex
almost as blatantly as it sells vodka. The woman is scantily
clothed, and the tray holding the bottle of vodka and plate
of fruit slices is strategically placed to call attention to her
genital area, both emphasizing society's value on sexuality.
The camera shoots a low angle shot of the woman (the
camera is placed below the woman), and combined with
her pulling the man toward her by his tie, emphasize the
woman's dominance in the scene. It appears that Cosmopolitan readers value women as sexual aggressors. The bright
lighting suggests fun and excitement. Together the visual images
place value on sex, passion and female dominance. The mood
would be much more romantic if the lighting were muted.

Another ad that makes the most out of lighting is a brightly lit ad for Vassarette from *Cosmopolitan* (Aug. 2002, p. 95). The model has a shy, seductive pose and is wearing a bright, magenta-colored Vassarette bra and bikini briefs. Her only item of street clothing is a pair of jeans, slung low on her hips showing virtually all of the briefs. The lighting, as well as the shy but seductive expression on the model's face, creates a happy and flirtatious mood. The low angle shot (in which the camera shoots from a spot lower than the woman's face) makes the woman and her underwear important. At the same time, it is also a straight on shot of her crotch, underscoring the importance of the sexual appeal. The shot, combined with the copy that alludes to sexual activity, further reinforces the importance of sexuality, and, also, the woman as sexual aggressor. The ad includes no description of the product features. Rather, it is a straightforward appeal to sex.

In contrast, many ads sell companionship and fun. The ad for Bud Light from *Cosmopolitan* (Aug., 2002, p. 151) sells good times and friends. These people are intimately close to each other. Bright lighting underscores the happy, upbeat mood of the ad. The low-angle camera shot makes these people appear important. The ad also shows a cultural value on racial diversity by including a woman of color on the far right and a very fair blonde woman at the left. There is a combination of an uneven number of women and men, suggesting that women and men can go out to a bar together as just friends. The ad does describe a product feature—the 110 calories—not a surprising feature on which to focus in a women's magazine.

Now let's consider an ad for Rimmell lipstick that ran in *People* (Dec. 1, 2003, p. 112). A close-up shot frames the model's lips as the focus of the shot. Further, there is bright lighting, and the contrast between the model's dark red lips and her fair hair and skin makes her lips stand out. The combination of the low-angle shot (in which the camera is shooting from a position lower than the subject of the shot) with a close up shot accentuates the importance of the model's lips. The ad cites the product feature of lipstick to last for a long time. The ad elaborates by saying that the product may last for up to seven hours. Students of advertising call the phrase "up to" a "weasel word," because it allows an ad to "weasel out" of a claim. "Up to" seven hours could actually mean only one minute.

Lighting and camera angles are also important in a two-page GM ad from *Automobile* (Oct., 2003, pp. 24–25). A high camera angle and warm lighting draw the reader's attention to the sleeping and safe toddler in his car seat, holding his teddy bear. Showing the toddler asleep underscores the safety valued in the ad. The entire second page of the two-page spread describes the safety features of the car and suggests that readers of *Automobile* are far more interested in product features than, for example, the readers of *People*, in which the RAV4 ad appeared. This ad combines the emotional appeal of the toddler with the rational appeal of the information about the safety of the product to sell GM.

Lighting and camera angles are also important in the ad for Walt Disney World from *Ebony* (Jan., 2004, p. 37), in which a family vacations at Disney World. A low camera angle frames the family and gives it importance, and the bright lighting shows readers that a family at Disney World will enjoy a good time. The smiles emphasize the happy experience. The ad also suggests a value on extended families—there appear to be grandparents at the right side of the page, and partial faces of people at the far right could be uncles, aunts or family friends. Although most of the models have dark skin, the mom, who is in the center of the shot, has straight hair and relatively light skin, again suggesting a societal preference for Caucasion features. Further, the woman who appears to be the grandmother also has straight hair. Furthermore, the woman who appears to be the grandmother has also straightened her hair. The fact that both of the adult women in the picture have straightened hair suggests this as the cultural preference for beauty. The product features mentioned include thrilling rides and enchantment, but the emotional appeal of family is central to the ad.

Commercials on Television

Television commercials communicate messages in all the ways magazine ads do—and more. In addition to the impact of lighting, camera angles, close up shots, choices of characters, editing carries a good deal of meaning in TV commercials. For example, fast cuts, in which one image replaces another in very rapid succession, along with bright lighting, make a toy like the Supersoaker water gun look terrifically exciting. Fast cuts and canted camera angles (in which the horizon is tilted) can also make the Chuck E. Cheese game arcade/restaurant seem to give the kids at a birthday party a thrill a minute. A toy like Laser Challenge, which kids use to shoot laser beams at each other, becomes thrilling and even dangerous with fast cuts between shots.

Commercials grab viewers' attention using digital editing, which creates special effects such as images that turn like the pages of a book or fly off the screen. A TV spot for a cereal such as French Toast Crunch uses digital editing to make the cereal box explode; this implies that eating the cereal creates excitement. A Fruit Gusher spot where kids' heads explode while they perform magic and eat Fruit Gushers, also suggests that eating Fruit Gushers will result in thrills. Computer enhancement along with sound effects make the Star Wars action figures look as though they can really act—the slogan, "Blast them before they blast you," suggests the plastic figures will really do something.

In addition, the products shown perform flawlessly— often even better than they really can. A spot for Workout

Barbie includes the disclaimer that the dolls can't really work out by themselves. But the editing makes Barbie look remarkably as if she's doing the workout by herself. Remote-controlled cars and planes don't accidentally crash, and playing with them seems to be like really flying. Commercials for craft items have also been enhanced. The girls use the Precious Metals Jewelry making kit to create wonderful items that girls at home are not likely to create. Directors reshoot or edit out any flawed performance, and special effects and sound effects enhance the illusion of reality.

Furthermore, celebrity endorsements let the viewer believe that the use of a product will win them the qualities of the celebrity. When basketball stars endorse Nike, viewers are urged to believe that wearing the shoe will make them better basketball players.

Just as ads in magazines sell emotions, television commercials do as well. Ads for fast food restaurants show families together, eating at a table in a relaxed happy mood. The ad is selling "family time," but in reality, whole families rarely eat as a family in fast food restaurants, and if they do, they are generally in a hurry, not in relaxed conversation.

Analyzing Television Programs

The same techniques used in commercials can be analyzed in television programs. Camera angles and lighting carry the same meaning on TV programs as in TV commercials and magazine ads. Low-angle shots give the subject of the shot power; high-angle shots make the subject weak. Canted-angle shots (in which the horizon is tilted) give an image of power and dynamism. A show like *America's Most Wanted*, for example, uses canted-angle shots to create a feeling of frenzy and disorientation.

Editing carries the same meaning on a TV show as in a TV commercial. A show like *COPS* has many quick edits which create intensity and urgency in the program. On the other hand, holding a single image on the screen for a long period of time lends calmness and perhaps romance.

Sound effects and music reinforce the physical aspects of a shot. Colossal claps of thunder, added to the image of a gray sky, tells viewers of an impending storm. The addition of whistling wind to a snowstorm means that the storm will turn dangerous. Country music makes a bar scene very different from one that uses jazz. Music can make a neutral scene seem happy or scary and dangerous. It can also divert viewers' attention from the visual images on the screen. Watch a music video with the volume muted. Without the distraction of the music, you may be alarmed at the number of sexual and violent images. Editors also modify the audio. Many sitcoms, even those taped before a live audience, "sweeten" the audio with the addition of a laugh track. The laugh track gets viewers to laugh at even the lamest humor.

Conventional Media Techniques

Television programs have conventions for both language and grammar. Various shots tell us different things. A fast zoom into a close-up shot calls the viewer's attention to the object of the shot. Perhaps it tells viewers that the person in the shot is the villain. A dissolve, in which one shot overlaps a second shot in the transition from shot to shot, tells viewers that a change in time or place has happened. For example, a dissolve from a shot of a romantic couple in a restaurant to a shot of them on a sofa means that they have left the restaurant and perhaps gone to an apartment. A fade to black means a major segment has ended. The screen fades to black just before a commercial break, for example.

Theme music, titles and graphics mark the opening and closing of a TV program. Usually the opening of an episode in a continuing series begins with a recap of last week's ending. Typically, shows break for commercials just at an exciting build up to ensure that viewers will stay tuned and watch the commercial.

In addition to conventions of television, newspapers also have conventions. The headline at the top of the front page indicates the most important story. The size of the font of the headline indicates the story's importance. Indeed, the largest font a newspaper uses is referred to by some journalists as "The Second Coming," indicating that a story is virtually as important as the Second Coming of Christ. More prominent stories are on the top half of the front page compared to the bottom half. Newspapers are arranged in sections for hard news, features, entertainment and sports, for example. And, the photographs used often carry emotional connotations to encourage readers to read the accompanying story.

Media Reinforce Cultural Values

The writers and producers of the media have points of view, backgrounds and values that influence their work. For the most part these people are affluent, White men who, in turn, influence American culture.

Look at *The Cosby Show* and notice the conspicuous consumption. Their kitchen contains virtually every appliance known to man. Cliff and Theo wear sumptuous sweaters and are never seen in the same one twice. Or look at the wealth implied in *Friends*. In reality, given the occupations of those characters, it would not be possible to live in and furnish their New York apartments. To the degree that television shapes kids' views about reality, many kids may feel that their own standard of living is inferior.

On TV, far more people have glamorous jobs than real-life people do. Television features attorneys, doctors and other professionals. TV programs rarely, if ever, feature grocery store checkout persons or bus boys as the main characters. Television programs also rarely show characters actually working. If characters do work, it is glamorous work. Attorneys, for example, aren't shown doing research in a law library. Rather, they argue colossal cases in jammed courtrooms. Again, kids may come to expect that it is very likely that they will become professionals who spend very little time actually working. Furthermore, they may anticipate that the work that they will do will be exciting and glamorous.

The messages on television and in teen magazines tell girls that they've got to be beautiful and thin, have boyfriends and be sexually active to be happy. The covers of teen magazines hype "hair rescue techniques," "twenty unbelievably easy slim-down ideas," "the 48-hour love upgrade," and "ways to instantly improve your sex life." This cultural value on appearance and sexuality puts pressure on girls to focus on these rather than inner qualities such as integrity or loyalty.

Another cultural value presented on TV concerns problem solving. Compromise is rarely shown as the preferred technique for solving problems. More often, force or violence ends disputes. Especially in cartoons, violence prevails. *The Powerpuff Girls* take on the problems of the world using violence. They attack the enemy, punching jaws and kicking victims, and viewers see blood and teeth fly across the screen. Buttercup throws fire, and Blossom throws lightening bolts to save the people of Townsville. These portrayals suggest to viewers that violence is an acceptable way to solve problems.

In spite of the strides of the women's movement, the media still prefers and values White men. White men outnumber women and people of color on dramatic programming as well as news. News, for example, rarely seeks out women as experts for hard news stories.[7]

Media messages have many layers, and you need to help

your children "deconstruct" them — and become media literate.

—What You Can Do—

- Talk with your children about the commercial nature of the media. Be sure they know that viewers are the products being delivered to sponsors.

- Discuss what features and feelings are being sold by commercials. Do this for both televised and print media.

- Videotape programs your children watch so that you can "deconstruct" them with your children —that is, carefully discuss the elements of production and how they contribute to the program. Then:

    Ask them how the lighting affects the story.

    Talk to them about the camera angles used and what they mean.

    Discuss the use of various camera shots—close ups, long shots, and what they mean.

    Discuss the use of music and sound effects. How do they affect the story?

    Watch a music video with the sound muted. Ask your children to describe the visual images.

    Count the number and rate of edits. What do they contribute to the program?

- Compare the news coverage of several media about the same story. How is *Hard Copy* or *Inside Edition* different from a newscast on the major networks? How is it different from newspaper coverage?

- Be aware that people of various ages and backgrounds process media messages differently. What you find entertaining, your eight-year-old may find terrifying. If you and your children are watching something that you find offensive, talk back to your TV set. Let your children know how you feel. Remind them that just because something is shown in the media, it's not necessarily the right thing to do.

- Discuss the values that are subtly presented. What kinds of people, objects and activities are presented positively? What is portrayed negatively?

- Ask your children how realistic the television people, settings and events are.

- Have your children write and produce a short television program. Ask them what kind of a commercial would fit with their show. Encourage them to experiment with the production techniques discussed in this chapter and talk about what they mean in their program. If you currently don't have access to a video camera, this might be a good excuse to get one.

- Several organizations produce media literacy materials for parents. They all have websites. Some of them are:

   Center for Media Literacy, www.medialit.org

   Center for Media Education, www.cme.org

   Media Education Foundation,
   www.mediaed.org

   KIDSNET, www.kidsnet.org

   PBS Kids, www.pbs.org/kids

- There are also several excellent films dealing with media literacy. They are probably available at your public library or at a video rental store. These are most appropriate for adult viewing. Watch them and talk about these media issues with your children.

Some of them are:

>   *Dream Worlds,* about the portrayal of women in the media

>   *Killing Screens*, about media violence

>   *The Ad & the Ego*, about advertising's cultural impact

>   *Tough Guise*, about the violent portrayal of men in the media

>   *Killing Us Softly*, about how advertising contributes to women's perceptions of beauty

>   *Mickey Mouse Monopoly*, about the impact of Disney films on culture

>   *Slim Hopes*, about advertising and eating disorders in women

Notes

Introduction

1. "Does Television Kill?" *Frontline*, narr. Bill Moyers, PBS, 10 Jan. 1995.

2. Kaiser Family Foundation, *Kids & Media @ the New Millennium* (Menlo Park CA: Author, 1999) 8.

3. Kaiser Family Foundation, *Kids & Media @ the New Millennium* (Menlo Park CA: Author, 1999) 6–7.

4. B. Lowry, "Company Town," *Los Angeles Times,* 9 Aug. 2001: C6.

5. Kaiser Family Foundation, *Kids & Media @ the New Millennium* (Menlo Park CA: Author, 1999) 11.

6. B. Gunter, "The Question of Media Violence," in *Media Effects: Advances in Theory and Research*, eds. J. Bryant and D. Zillman (Hillsdale NJ: Erlbaum, 1994) 163-212.

7. M. Schorr. (2001, Sept. 11). *We Like To Watch*. Retrieved October 14, 2002, from http://abcnews.go.com/sections/living/DailyNews/violenceresearch000911.html

8. Schorr.

9. M. Clary, "Boy 14 Gets Life Term in Wrestling Killing," *Los Angeles Times,* 2001 Mar. 10: A1.

10. B. Clark, interview with Terry Gross, *Fresh Air*, Nat'l Public Radio, WHYY, Philadelphia, 27 May 1996.

11. M. McCombs, "News Influence on Our Pictures of the World," *Media Effects: Advances in Theory and Research*, eds. J. Bryant, and D. Zillman (Hillsdale NJ: Erlbaum, 1994) 1-16.

12. P. Cram, S. Vijan, M.E. Cowen, D. Carpenter, and A.M. Fendrick, "The Impact of a Celebrity Spokesperson on Preventive Health Behavior: The Katie Couric Effect," *Society of General Internal Medicine Meeting*, Atlanta GA, 2002 May 3.

13. "Overall We'll Miss Oprah's Book Club," *Pittsburgh Post Gazette*, 2002 April 3: G8.

14. "Poll Finds Strong 'Nag Factor' in Children," *Chicago Tribune*, 2002 June 28: Sec 1: 10.

Chapter 1

1. Dr. Joyce Brothers, "If You Want to be a Better Parent . . . Here are the TV Moms and Dads You Should Learn From," *TV Guide*, 1989 Mar. 4, 21-25.

2. R. Zoglin, "Home is Where the Venom is," *Time*, 1990 Apr. 1990, 85-86.

3. M. Larson, "Family Communication on Prime-Time Television," *Journal of Broadcasting & Electronic Media* 37.3 (1993): 349-357.

4. M. Larson, "Sex Roles and Soap Operas: What Adolescents Learn About Single Motherhood," *Sex Roles* 35.1/2 (1996): 97-110.

5. National Commission on Working Women, *Women, work and family: Working mothers-overview* (Washington D.C: Author, (1991-1992).

6. J. Robinson, and T. Skill, "Five Decades of Families on Television: From the 1950s Through the 1990s," *Television and the American Family*, 2nd ed., ed. J. Bryant, and A. Bryant (Mahwah NJ: Erlbaum, 2001) 139-162.

7. Robinson and Skill.

8. Robinson and Skill.

9. The TV Single Dad Hall of Fame. Retrieved 2002 Sep. 24, from http://www.tvdads.com/tvdad.html

10. M. Larson, "Family Communication on Prime-Time Television," *Journal of Broadcasting & Electronic Media* 37.3 (1993): 349-357.

11. *The Oprah Show*, 2002 Sept. 4.

12. S. Bank and M. Kahn, "Sisterhood-brotherhood is Powerful: Sibling Subsystems and Family Therapy," *Family Process* 14 (1975): 311-337.

13. M. Larson, "Sibling Interaction in Situation Comedies Over the Years," in *Television and the American Family*, eds. J. Bryant and A. Bryant, 2nd ed. (Mahwah NJ: Erlbaum, 2001) 163-176.

14. M. Larson, "Sibling Interactions in 1950s versus 1980s sitcoms: A Comparison," *Journalism Quarterly* 68.3 (1991): 381-387.

15. M. Larson, "Sibling Interaction in Situation Comedies."

16. L. Heffley, "Telly Trouble?" *Los Angeles Times,* 1998 Apr. 4, home ed.: F1.

17. S. Cohen, "Television in the Lives of Children and Their Families," *Childhood Education,* 1993.94: 103-104.

18. Kaiser Family Foundation, *Kids & Media @ the New Millennium* (Menlo Park CA: Author, 1999) 8.

Chapter 2

1. A. Marks, "TV and Toy Trend Affects Young Children," *Christian Science Monitor,* 7 May 1996, p1, 1c.

2. R. Stodghill, "Where'd You Learn That?" *Time,* 1998 June 15, 50-59.

3. Marks.

4. V. Strasburger. (n.d.). Getting Your Kids to say "No" in the New Millennium When You Said "Yes" in the Last Millennium. Retrieved 2002 Oct. 8, from http://healthology.com/ focus_article.asp?f=teenhealth&c+teen_sayingno

5. Stodghill.

6. K. Lichtenberg. (1999). Recent TV Dating Games Have Surpassed Idiocy. Retrieved 2002 July 3, from wysiwyg://149http:/ Kendrick.colgate.edu . . .archivesS99/021299/commentary/dating.html

7. S. Kummerer, "MTV's *Singled Out*: Dating Reality or Dangerous Role Model?" Unpublished paper, Northern Illinois University, 1998.

8. C. Woolery, interview with Todd Mundt, *The Todd Mundt Show,* Nat'l. Public Radio, Michigan Public Radio, Ann Arbor, 2002 Oct. 24.

9. Kaiser Family Foundation, *Sex on TV: News Release* (Menlo Park CA: 2001).

10. J. Leo, "Raging Hormones on TV," *U.S. News & World Report,* 1998 2 Feb. 9.

11. L. M. Ward, "Talking About Sex: Common Themes About Sexuality in Prime-Time Television Programs Children and Adolescents View Most," *Journal of Youth and Adolescence* 24 (1995): 595-615.

12. Kaiser Family Foundation, 2001.

13. Kaiser Family Foundation, 2001.

14. J. Gallagher. (1998 April 14). Ellen DeGeneres: "We're not coming back." Retrieved 2002 Nov. 11, from http://www.findarticles.com

15. Alliance for Traditional Marriage and Values. (2001 May 31). Pro-Family Supporters Outraged as the WB Network's *Dawson's Creek* Promotes Homosexuality to Teens. Retrieved 2002 Nov. 13 from http:// 222.sphi.com/pressreleases/0006/supporters_outrage.htm

16. abcnews. (2001). Oh Boy . . . *Dawson's Creek* Stirs Debate with Gay Kiss. Retrieved 2002 Nov. 13, from http://abcnews.go.com/sections/entertainment/Daily News/dawsonskiss010501.html

17. J. Portner, "Homosexual Students: A Group Particularly Vulnerable to Suicide," *Education Week* 19 (2000): 32.

18. Portner.

19. C. Torres. (n.d.). Searching for a Way Out: Stopping Gay Teen Suicide. Retrieved 2002 Nov. 12, from http://www.healthyplace.com/Communities/Gender/gayisok/stopping_suicide.html

20. A. Kielwasser and M. Wolf, "Mainstream Television, Adolescent Homosexuality, and Significant Silence," *Critical Studies in Mass Communication* 9 (1992): 350-373.

21. American Academy of Pediatrics. (2001 July). Sexuality, Contraception and the Media (RE0038). Retrieved 2002 Oct. 8, from http://aap.org/policy/re0038.html

22. Putting the Pieces Together. (2001). Retrieved 2002 Oct. 8, from http://www.teenweb.org/teens.phpe?p_id67&section=29

23. Strasburger.

24. Kaiser Family Foundation, 2001.

25. American Academy of Pediatrics.

26. Factoids: Teen Pregnancy. (2002, April 23). Retrieved 2002 Oct. 1, from http://www.youthnoise.com/site/CDA/CDA Page0,1004,816,00.html

27. "Health Kick: You Oughta Know," *Cosmogirl, 2002* Aug.: 104.

28. "50 Worst Shows of All Time," *TV Guide,* 2002 July 20-26: 12-28.

29. Kaiser Family Foundation, *Sex on TV* (Menlo Park CA: 1999).

30. Kaiser Family Foundation, *Teens, Sex and TV* (Menlo Park CA: 2002 May).

31. J. Check, "Teenage Training: The Effects of Pornography on Adolescent Males," *The Price We Pay,* ed. L. Lederer and R. Delgado ((NY: Hill and Wang, 1995) 89-91.

32. Stodghill.

33. "Sex and the Suburbs," *Cosmogirl,* 2002 Aug.: 176-177.

34. M. Burford, "Girls and Sex: You Won't Believe What's Going On," *O: The Oprah Magazine,* 2002 Nov.: 212-215.

35. Stodghill.

36. D. Wood, "Helping Teenagers Develop Criteria for Deciding When It Is Right To Have Sex," Paper presented at the Annual Meeting of the American School Health Association, St. Louis, MO, 1996, Oct. 30-Nov.

(ERIC Documentation Reproduction Service No. ED403262)

37. Stodghill.

38. T. Eng, "The Hidden Epidemic," Issues in Science and Technology, 13 (1997, Summer): 80-81.

39. Factoids.

40. A. Mulrine, "Risky Business," *U.S. News & World Report, 2002* May 27: 42-49.

41. Stodghill, 50-59.

42. M. Daly, "Talk to Me," Cosmogirl, 2002 Aug., 134-135.

43. Stodghill.

44. Daly.

45. Daly.

46. "Adolescent Sexual Health in Europe and the U.S.—Why the Difference," *Advocates for Youth,* 2001 Oct. and 2003 May 4, http://www.advocatesfor youth.org/publications/factsheet/fsest.htm

47. Strasburger.

48. Ask Anabelle. (1998). Retrieved 2002 Oct. 3, from http://www.angelfire.com/ca5/Annabelle/rjan0019.html

Chapter 3

1. M. Clary, "Boy, 14, Gets Life Term in Wrestling Killing; Courts: He Was Imitating WWF When Playmate Died, Defense Said. Prosecutor Supports Bid For Clemency," *Los Angeles Times* 2001 Mar. 10, Part A, Part 1, P. 1

2. abcnews. (2001 Jan. 29). *Jackass* Imitation Stunt: Boy Recovering After Imitating MTV Show Stunt. Retrieved from http://abcnews.go.com/sections/us/DailyNews/jackass-burning010129.html

3. Committee on Public Education, 2000-2001, "Media Violence," *Pediatrics* 108 (2001): 1222-1226.

4. T. Williams. *The Impact of Television* (New York: Academic Press, 1986).

5. M. Schorr. (2000 Sept. 11). We Like to Watch: Violent Media and Violent Behavior. Retrieved 2002 Oct. 14 from http://abcnews.go.com/sections/living/DailyNews/violenceresearch000911.html

6. D. Levin. *Remote Control Childhood?* (Washington DC: National Association for the Education of Young Children, 1998). (p. 13)

7. D. Lavers, "The Verdict on Media Violence: It's Ugly. . .and Getting Uglier," *Insight on the News*, 2002 May 13: 28.

8. Lavers.

9. M. Young. (2001 Feb. 6). Children Awash in Images That Make Them Think Violence is Cool and the World is Scary. Retrieved from http://hardnewscafe.usu/archive/feb2001/0206_violence3.html

10. J. Rutenberg, "Violence Finds a Niche in Children's Cartoons," *New York Times* 2001 Jan. 28, Late Edition: sec. 1, p. 1.

11. Committee on Public Education.

12. A. Dickinson, "Violent Cartoons: Should *The Lion King* be Rated PG?" *Time,* 2000 June 12: 90.

13. Children Now. (Winter 1998). Children and Television Violence. Retrieved 2003 Jan. 17, from http://www.childrennow.org/media/medianow/mnwinter1998.html

14. M. Larson, "Gender, Race, and Aggression in Television Commercials That Feature Children," *Sex Roles: A Journal of Research* 48.1/2 (2003): 67-75.

15. Committee on Communications, "Impact of Music Lyrics and Music Videos on Children and Youth," *Pediatrics* 98.6 (1996): 1219-1221.

16. Eminem Lyrics (n.d.). Kill You. Retrieved 2003 Feb. 27, from http://www.azlyrics.com/lyrics/eminem/killyou.html

17. Andrew W.K. Lyrics (n.d.). Ready to Die. Retrieved 2003 Feb. 27, from http://www.azlyrics,com/lyrics/andrewwk/readytodie.html

18. R. Lichter, L. Lichter, and D. Amundson. (June 1999). Merchandizing Mayhem: Violence in Popular Entertainment. Retrieved 2003 Feb. 25, from http://www.cmpa.coom/archive/viol98.htm

19. P. Latham, "The Blood and Violence Are Real," *Cox News Service* 2002 Dec. 23: Commentary. (Marshall News-Messenger)

20. L. Holmes. (1998). Watching Wrestling Positively Associated With Date Fighting. Retrieved from http://mentalheatlh.about.com.library/sci/0401/blwrestle401.htm?terms=television

21. (n.d.) The Best of Backyard Wrestling Videos. Retrieved from http://www.backyardwrestlingvideos.com/

22. D. Linz, and E. Donnerstein, "Sex and Violence in Slasher Films: A Reinterpretation," Journal of Broadcasting & Electronic Media 38.2 (1994): 243-246.

23. J. Cantor, *Mommy, I'm Scared,* (San Diego: Harcourt Brace & Company, 1998), 112.

24. Larson.

25. Lavers.

26. T. Johnson, "The Decline of Television's Family Hour," *USA Today,* 1996 Nov. 1: 60-2.

27. Parents Television Council. (n.d.). Take Action Now! Retrieved

from http://www.parentstv.org/actionalert/actiongoldenglobes.asp

28. J. Rutenberg, "Few Viewers Object as Unbleeped Bleep Words Spread on Network TV," *New York Times*, 2003 Jan. 25, B7.

29. APA HelpCenter (n.d.). Family and Relationships: Get the Facts. Retrieved 2003 Feb. 8, from http://helping.apa.org/family/kidtvviol.html

30. D. Germain. (2000 May 23). Deceptively Innocent. Study: G-rated Carton Flicks Surprisingly Violent. Retrieved 2003 Feb. 4, from http://abcnews.go.com/sections/living/DailyNews/violence0523.html

31. APA HelpCenter.

32. R. Morin, "Before Saying 'I do,' ask, 'Are you a *Roadrunner* fan?'" *Washington Post* 2002 May 28, A3.

33. Mediascope (2000). Youth and Violent Music. Retrieved 2003 Jan. 29, from http://www.mediascope.org/pubs/ibriefs/yvm.htm

34. D. Lemish, "The School as a Wrestling Arena: The Modelling of a Television Series," *Communication* 22 (1997): 395-418.

35. L. Bozell III. (1999 Aug. 5). Skimpy Clothing, Sex Aplenty, But It's Not the Daytime Soaps. Retrieved from http://secure.mediaresearch.org/columns/ent/coll9990805.html

36. V. Smith. (2001, August). Excerpt From "Someone Has to Say Enough" Submission to the Standing Committee on Canadian Heritage, Study on the State of Canadian Broadcasting. Retrieved 2003 Jan. 19, from http://bicp.org/vswwf.html

37. P. Webster, "French Link Murders to Cult Film: 'Scream' Blamed for Outbreak of Teenage Violence," *The Observer* 2002 June 9. Retrieved 2003 Jan. 20, from http://www.fradical.com/Scream_related_murder.htm

38. B. Olson. (2002 Aug. 8). New Research Study Says Kids Who Watch Violent Media are Rude, Mean and Carry a Chip on Their Shoulders. Retrieved 2003 Feb. 8, from http://www.mediafamily.org/press/20020808-1.shtml

39. D. Linz, E. Donnerstein, and S. Penrod, "The Effects ofMultiple Exposures to Filmed Violence Against Women," *Journal of Communication* 34 (1984): 130-147.

40. Webster.

41. Holmes.

42. Committee on Public Education, 2000-2001, "Media Violence," *Pediatrics* 108 (2001): 1222-1226.

43. Cantor.

45. J. Cantor, and A. Nathanson, "Children's Fright Reactions to Television News," *Journal of Communication* 46.4 (1996): 139-152.

Chapter 4

1. S. McClelland, "Distorted Images," *Maclean's* 113: 33 (2000Aug. 14): 41-42.

2. J. Wheldon, "Agenda 2002: Study Links TV to Eating Disorders," *Belfast News Letter* 2002 June 1, p. 4.

3. McClelland.

4. J. Zimmerman, "An Image to Heal," *Humanist* 57: 1 (1997, Jan.): 20-25.

5. A. Young, "Battling Anorexia: The Story of Karen Carpenter," *Mind & Body* (n.d.) 2003 July 1, http://atdpweb.soe.berkeley.edu/quest/Mind&Body/Carpenter.html

6. M. Errico, "Calista Collapses!" *E! Online* 2000 Dec. 15, 2003 July 2, http://www.eonline.com/News/Items/0,1,7529,00.html

7. "Tracey Gold Discusses Her Struggle with Anorexia," *Dateline NBC,* 1999 Mar. 1, 2003 July 2, http://eatingdisorderresources.com/tv/datelinenbc030199traceygold.html

8. "'Soprano's Star Tells of Anorexia Battle,'" *CBSNEWS.com* 2002 Aug. 19, 2003 July 2, http://www.cbsnews.com/stories/2002/08/19/earlyshow/leisure/books/printable519147.shtml

9. K. Schneider, "Mission Impossible," *People Weekly* 45 (1996 June 3): 64-68.

10. Schneider.

11. "Media Influence on Eating Disorders," *Rader Programs,* 2003 June, 2003 July 2, http://www.raderprograms.com/media.htm

12. C. Brabbs, "Adland confused over 'waif' code," *Marketing,* 2000 June 29: 7.

13. S. Hall, "Obsession for Men," *New York Times Upfront,* 2000 Feb.14, 12-15.

14. Schneider.

15. J. Smolowe, "Everything to Lose," *People* 58: 19 (4 Nov. 2002): 58-63.

16. Smolowe.

17. Z. Hughes, "What to do if Your Child is Too Fat," *Ebony* 55: 9 (2000 July): 96-100.

18. C. Mithers, "From Baby Fat to Obesity," *Parenting* 15: 8 (2001 October): 108-115.

19. K. Davis, "How to Raise Healthy Children," *Ebony* 56: 9 (2001 July): 44-46.

20. "Healthy Weight Benefits," *Blubber Busters School* 2002, 2003 July 2, http://blubberbuster.com/school/benefits.htm

21. Mithers.

22. M. Slatalla, "Keep 'em Moving," *Time* 156: 1 (2000 July 3): 66.

23. D. Halonen, "Group Seeks Curbs on Kids Advertising," *Advertising Age* 71: 44 (2000 Oct. 23): 93.

24. Congressional Briefing, "Facts About the Effects of Advertising and Marketing on Children," *Stop Commercial Exploitation of Children* (n.d.), 2003 April 16, http://www.commercialexploitation.com/articles/congressional_briefing_facts.htm

25. Mithers.

26. "Black Children Eat Most of Their Meals While Watching TV," *Jet* 99: 13 (2001 March 12): 18.

27. "An Ample Market," *Chain Store* 78: 9 (2002 Sept.): 42.

28. D. Dolan, "The Kindest Cut? Teens and Plastic Surgery," *The New York Observer* 2003 March 3, 2003 July 1 2003. http://observer.com/pages/youth.asp

29. Dolan.

30. "Looking Like a Celebrity," *abc NEWS.com* 2002 March 27, 2003 July 17 http://abcnews.go.com/sections/Downtown/2020/Downtown_020327_plasticsurgery_feature.html

31. J. Restivo, "Asset Enhancement," *abc NEWS.com* 2001 Jan. 29, 2003 July 17 http://abcnews.go.com/sections/living/GoodMorningAmerica/lopezlift_020129.html

32. "ABC 'Downtown' Exclusive!" *ET Celebrities* 2002 March 27, 2003 July 17 http:www.etonline.com/celebrity/a9744.htm

33. H. Kotbe, "Quest for the Perfect Body Starts Young," *MSNBC News*, 2002 July 28, 2003 May 10 2003 http://www.msnbc.com/news/382325.asp

34. J. Frankel, "Teens Hot for Surgical Looks," *CBSNews.com* 29 Oct. 1999, 2003 July 12, http://www.cbsnews.com/stories/1999/10/29/earlyshow/living/parenting/printable37640.shtml

35. Dolan.

36. M. Hardcastle, "Body Image: A Pep Talk," *Teen Advice*, 2000 June 3, 2003 July 3 2003 http://teenadvice.about.com/library/weekly/aa060300a.htm

37. M. Larson, "Health-Related Messages Embedded in Prime-Time Television Entertainment," *Health Communication* 3: 3 (1991): 175-184.

38. D. Roberts and P. Christenson, "'Here's Looking at You, Kid:' Alcohol, Drugs and Tobacco in Entertainment Media," (Menlo Park, CA: Kaiser Family Foundation, 2000 Feb.).

39. H. Hundley, "The Naturalization of Beer in *Cheers,*" *Journal of Broadcasting & Electronic Media* 39: 3 (1995): 350-359.

40. E. Weintraub and H. Meili, "Effects of Interpretations of Televised Alcohol Portrayal on Children's Alcohol Beliefs," *Journal of Broadcasting & Electronic Media* 38: 4 (1994): 417-443.

41. Roberts and Christenson.

42. K. Thompson and F. Yokota, "Depiction of Alcohol, Tobacco and Other Substances in G-rated Animated Feature Films," *Pediatrics* 107: 2001 June 6): 1369-1374.

43. M. Rich, "For a Child, Every Moment is a Teachable Moment," *Pediatrics* 108 (2001 July): 179-180.

44. Roberts and Christenson.

45. "Stars Smoking in Films and TV: A 1998 Report on Smoking in the Movies," TobaccoFree.org 2003, 2003 July 6, *http://www.tobaccofree.org/films.htm*

46. Thompson and Yokota.

47. Roberts and Christenson.

48. E. Ross, "Study Faults Films for Teens' Smoking," *newsobserver.com* 2003 June 9, 2003 July 6, http://newsobserver.com/24hour/science/story/912534p-6356069c.html

49. Roberts and Christenson.

50. Roberts and Christenson.

51. L. Krieger, "Shh! All the Noise Leaves Us Dragging," *Chicago Tribune* 9, 1990 Nov. 9, A25.

52. P. Gott, "Noise-deafness is Preventable; Trouble Digesting Fats," *Jewish World Review*, 2001 Sept. 14, 2003 July 9 http://www.jewishworldreview.com/cols/gott091401.asp

53. Krieger.

54. "Noise Affects Children's Hearing," *Audiological Consultants of Atlanta* (n.d.), 2003 April 19, http://www.audioconsult.com/kidnoise.html

55. "Music Induced Hearing Loss is a Growing Problem," *Hearing Depot.com* 2000 May, 2003 July 1 http://www.hearingcenteronline.com/newsletter/may00x.shtml

56. D. Daniel, "Earplugs Rock," *Boston Globe*, 1997 July 25, C1.

57. "Famous Boomers with Significant Hearing Loss and/or Tinnitus," hear-it (n.d.), 2003 July 10, http://www.hear-it.org/page.dsp?page=2649

58. B. Picture, "H.E.A.R. and Now! Loud Clubs and Hearing Loss," *H.E.A.R.* 2002 Feb. 24, 2003 July 10. http://www.hearnet.com/about/about_press_hereandnow.shtml

59. "Music Induced."

60. S. Lang, "Computers in Schools are Putting Elementary Schoolchildren at Risk for Posture Problems, Says Cornell Study," *Cornell News* 1999 Feb.1, 2003 March 8, http://www.news.cornell.edu/releases/Feb99/kids.computers.ssl.html

61. "Computers," *HealthyComputing.com* 2001, 2003 Mar. 25, http://www.healthycomputing.com/kids/computers.html

62. K. Kashmanian, "The Impact of Computers on Schools: Two Authors, Two Perspectives," *The Technology Source*, 2000 July/Aug. Available online at http://ts.mivu.org/default.asp?shoow=article&id=791. Retrieved 2003 Mar. 1.

63. J. VanTine, "Protect Computer Wizards from Joint Problems," *Prevention* 51.3 (1999 Mar.): 36.

64. R. Senior, "Not Just Fun and Games," *Advance for Physical Therapists& PT Assistants* 14.13 (2003 June 9): 8-10. 65.

Chapter 5

1. C. Barney, "Kids' Channels Beat Networks to Diversity," *The San Diego Union-Tribune*, 2002 Aug. 2003: E-5.

2. S. Douglas, "We've Come a Long Way. Maybe," *M 6.3* (1995 Nov.): 76-80.

3. A. Billen, "Girl Power," *New Statesman* 14.654 (2002 April 23): 46.

4. K. Fry, "Maude: U.S. Situation Comedy," *Maude* (n.d.), 2003 Sept. 11, http://www.museum.tv/archives/etv/M/htmlM/maude/maude.htm

5. *Three's Company: U.S. Situation Comedy* (n.d.) 2003 Sept. 18, http://www.museum.tv/archives/etv/T/htmlT/threescompa/threescopa.htm

6. T. Ramlow, "Charlie's Angels: The Complete First Season," *Pop Matters Television Review,* 2003 May 27, 2003 Sept. 18, http://popmatters.com/tv/reviews/c/charlies-angels-complete-season1.shtml

7. A. Billen, "Girl Power," *New Statesman* 14.654 (2001 April 23): 46.

8. *Cagney and Lacey: U.S. Police Series* (n.d.) 2003 Sept. 25, http://www.museum.tv/archives/etv/C/htmlC/cagneyandla/cagneyandla.htm

9. R. Wodell, "The Golden Girls: An Episode Guide," *Epguides.com*, 2003 May 4, 2003 Sept.13, http://epguides.com/GoldenGirls/guide.shtml

10. *Murhpy Brown: U.S. Situation Comedy* (n.d.) 2003 Sept. 27, http://www.museum.tv/archives/etv/M/htmlM/murphybrown/murphybrown.htm

11. J. Chidley, "The Most Famous Canadian on the Planet?: She is All Over TV and the Tabliods—everywhere. For Better or for Worse, Pamela Lee is Our Biggest Star," *Maclean's* 108 (1995 Nov. 27): 48-51.

12. J. Clausen and M. Kielbasa, "Of Myths and Mermaids: Nurturing the Spirituality of Adolescent Girls," *America* 185.8 (2001 Sept. 24): 20-23.

13. H. Giroux, "Are Disney Movies Good for Your Kids?" *Kinderculture,* eds. S. Steinberg and J. Kincheloe (Boulder CO: Westview Press, 1997) 53-67.

14. "Watch Out, Listen Up! 2002 Feminist Primetime Report," *National Organization for Women Foundation* (n.d.) 2003 Mar. 11, http:// www.nowfoundation.org/watchout3/index.html

15. "Headlines," *Headlines: February 2003 Archives,* 2003 Mar., 2003 Sept. 28, http://www.survivoramazon.com/archives/2003_02.php

16. M. Kingwell, "Buffy Slays Ally," *Saturday Night,* 113.4 (1998 May): 77-78.

17. F. Early, "Staking her Claim: Buffy the Vampire Slayer as Transgressive Woman Warrior," *Journal of Popular Culture* 35.3 (2001 Winter): 11-27.

18. T. Strauss, "A Manifesto for Third Wave Feminism," 2000 Oct. 24, 2003 Oct. 5, http://alternet.org/print.html?StoryID=9986

19. R. Fudge, "The Buffy Effect: Or a Tale of Cleavage and Marketing," *Bitch,* 1999 Summer, 2003 Oct. 2 http://www.bitchmagazine.com/ archives/08_01buffy/buffy1.htm

20. H. Havrilesky, "Powerpuff Girls Meet World," *Salon.com* 2002, 2003 July 2, 2002 Oct. 5, http://archive.salon.com/mwt/feature/2002/07/02/ powerpuff/print.html

21. "From Sailor Moon to Powerpuff Girls: Female Action Heroes," *Media Awareness Network* 2003, 2003 Oct. 5, http://www.media-awareness.ca/english/resources/educational/handouts/gender_portrayal/ action_heroes.cfm

22. K. Anderson and D. Cavallaro, "Parents or Pop Culture? Children's Heroes and Role Models," *Childhood Education* 78.3 (2002 Spring): 161-168.

23. "Watch Out, Listen Up! 2002 Feminist Primetime Report," *National Organization for Women Foundation* (n.d.) 2003 March 11, http:// www.nowfoundation.org/watchout3/index.html

24. "Science and Technology: Public Attitudes and Public Understanding," (n.d.) 2003 Jan. 24, http://www.nsf.gov/sbe/srs/seind02/pdf/c07.pdf

25. Children NOW, *Fall Colors: Prime Time Diversity Report* (Oakland CA: Author, 2002).

26. Children NOW, *Boys to Men: Messages about Masculinity* (Oakland CA: Author, 1999).

27. Giroux.

28. National Organization for Women Foundation, *Watch Out, Listen*

Up! (Washington D.C.: Author, 2002).

29. Children NOW, *A Different Light: Children's Perceptions of Race and Class in the Media* (Author, 2002).

30. F. McKissack, "The Problem with Black T.V.," *The Progressive* 61 (1997 Feb. : 38-40.

31. McKissack, "Television's Black Humor," *The Progressive* 63 (1999 Apr.): 39-40.

32. "Blacks 'ghettoized' on TV says SAG Report," *Jet* 98.5 (2000 July 10): 48.

33. H. Doby, "Networks to Bow to NAACP Heat," *Black Enterprise* 30.9 (2000 Apr.): 26.

34. "New Faces on TV," *Jet* 101.5 (2002 Jan. 21): 56-62.

35. T. Smith, "Cross-dressing in China, as Disney Would Have Us Believe," *The Daily,* 24 June 1998, 4 Feb. 2003 http://archives.the daily.washington.edu/1998/062498/mulan.6.23.html

36. Giroux.

37. "Latinos Hardly Visible on Prime-Time Television, UCLA Study Finds," *Black Issues in Higher Education* 20.7 (2003 May 22): 16.

38. R. Huff, "If Diversity Means More Latinos, TV's Doing Better," *The Miami Herald; Herald.com* 2003 Oct. 16, http://www.miami.com/mld/miamiherald/entertainment/7016808.htm

39. *Fall Colors.*

40. D. Whitney, "Hispanic Shows Making Prime-Time Progress," *Electronic Media* 21.47 (2002 Nov. 25): p. 10, 13.

41. D. Reese, "Mom, Look! It's George, and he's a TV Indian!" *The Horn Book* 74.5 (1998 Sept./Oct.): 636-643.

42. Children NOW, *Fall Colors: Prime Time Diversity Report* (Oakland CA: Author, 2002).

43. G. Braxton, "Coalition Laments the Invisibility of Asians, Native Americans on TV," *Los Angeles Times* 2003 Oct. 14: Business part 2, p. 3.

44. C. Campbell and L. Edmo-Suppah, "Television's Troubling Indian Images," *Television Quarterly* 33.4 (2003 Spring): 16-25.

45. T. Smith, "Cross-dressing in China, as Disney Would Have Us Believe," *The Daily,* 1998 June 24, 2003 Feb. 4 http://archives.the daily.washington.edu/1998/062498/mulan.6.23.html

46. M. Jacobson, "*Peter Pan:* Special Edition" 2002 Feb. 12, 2003 Nov. 11, http://www.dvdmoviecentral.com/ReviewsTExt/peter_pan_disney.htm

47. *Fall Colors.*

48. B. Lowry, "'Banzai'—a Controversy by Fox," *Los Angeles Times,* 2003 July 11: Part5: 34.

49. *"Banzai* Update: Sponsors Pull from 'Banzai' s Ratings Drop and Fox Censors their Message Board" (n.d.), 2003 Oct. 16 http:// www.manaa.org/articles/banzai_update.html

50. "Restrictive Portrayals of Asians in the Media and How to Balance Them," (n.d.), 2003 Oct. 16, http://www.manaa.org/articles/stereo.html

51. *Fall Colors.*

52. *Fall Colors.*

53. J. Shaheen, "Hollywood Widens Slur Targets to Arab and Muslim American Since Sept. 11," 2002 Feb. 27, 2003 Oct. 16, http:// news.nconline.com/news/view_article.html?article_id=820

54. E. Sauers, "Tuning in to the Inner Prejudice," *Indiana Daily Student* 23, 2003 Sept. 23, 2003 Oct. 16, http://idsnews.com/ story.php?id=18363

55. Smith.

56. Giroux.

57. Shaheen.

58. T. Feran, "But 'Invisible Minority' Makes Inroads," *Cleveland Plain Dealer,* 2000, 2003 Dec. 12, 2003 Sept. 1, , http://www.mult-sclerosos.org/ news /Dec2000/DisabledActors.html

59. Feran.

60. Feran.

61. C. Campbell and S. Hoem, "PrimeTime's Disabled Images," *Television Quarterly* 32.1 (2001 Spring): 44-40.

62. Christopher and Hoem.

63. Feran.

64. B. Acosta, "The Age of 'Honor'" *The Austin Chronicle Screens: TV Eye,* 2002 Oct. 11, 2003 Oct. 23, http://www.tvguide.ca/newsgossip-archives/02-sep/09-07-02.html

65. K. White, " Senior Actors Call on Hollywood to End Ageism," *Las Vegas Review-Journal: reviewjournal.com,* 2000, 2003 June 15, 2003 Oct. 19, http://www.lvj.com/cgi-bin/printable.cgi?/lvj_home/Jun-15-Thu-2000/ news/13780691.html

66. B. Briller, "TV's Distorted and Missing Images of Women and the Elderly," *Television Quarterly* 31.1(2000 Spring): 69-74.

67. "Seniors in Short Supply on Television," *Voice and Variety,* 2000 Oct., 2003 Oct. 19, http://www.srgvoice.com/images2/pdf/variety-oct 100.pdf

68. Briller.

69. White.

70. Briller.

71 Acosta.

Chapter 6

1. S. Begley, "Your Child's Brain," *Newsweek*, 1996 Feb.19: 54-58.

2. "Brain Development," *Smart Start and Brain Development* (n.d.), http://www.smartstart-nc.org/parents/brain.htm 2002 Nov. 29

3. K. Oliver. "Your Child's Brain: The First Crucial Years," *Ohio State University Extension Factsheet* (n.d.). http://ohioline.osu.edu/hygfact/5000/5318.html 2002 Nov. 29

4. J. Nash, "Fertile Minds," *Time*, 1997 Feb., 3, 48-56.

5. A. Matthews. "Media May Impact Children's Learning," *Mississipi State University*, 2001 Feb. 26, http://msucares.com/news/print/fcenews/fce01/010226.html 2003 March 1.

6. "Can Violent Media Affect Reasoning and Logical Thinking?" *Violent Media and Reasoning* (n.d.). http://www.sosparents.org/Brain percent20Study.htm 2003 March.

7. T. Cottle, "On TV and Teens, Brains and Rage," *Television Quarterly* 33. 2/3 (2002 Summer/Fall): 58-62.

8. Matthews.

9. S. Dunnewind, "TV or Not TV, That's the Question," *Houston Chronicle* 2002 June 24, star edition: 3

10. K. Bedford. "Pediatricians again advise against TV for very young kids," *Current Online*, 1999 Aug. 28, http://www.current.org/ch/ch915p.html 2003 March 29.

11. D. Bauder. "Sesame Street getting huge makeover," *Yahoo News*, 2002 Feb. 4, http://dailynews.yahoo.com/h/ap/20020204/en/ap_on_tv_sesame_street.html 2002 Feb. 7.

12. G. DeGaetano. "Visual Media and Young Children's Attention Spans," *Media Literacy Review* (n.d.) http://interact.uoregon.edu/MediaLit/mlr/readings/articles/degaetano/visualmedia.html , 2003 Mar. 12.

13. M. Dumont, "Focusing on Television," *American Journal of Psychiatry* 133 (1976 Apr.): 457.

14. G. Legwold, "Less TV, More Life," *Better Homes and Gardens*, 1998 Nov.: 110-112.

15. S. Boseley, "TV Exposure Damages Child Speech," *The Guardian*, 1996 Jan. 10: 1.

16. "Sharing Books with Babies," *ZERO TO THREE Brain Wonders*, (n.d.) http://www.zerotothree.org/brainwonders/EarlyLiteracy/chew.html 2003 Mar. 7.

17. B. Mates and L. Strommen, "Why Ernie Can't Read: *Sesame Street* and Literacy," *Reading Teacher* 49.4 (1995): 300-306.

18. L. Sax. "Ritalin: Better Living Through Chemistry?" *The World & I Online*, 2000 Nov. http://www.worldandi.com/public/2000/november/sax.html 2003 Mar. 7.

19. "Computers, TV, and Very Young Children: What Impact on Development?" *Zero to Three* (2001 Oct./Nov.: 30-33.

20. H. Cummins, "'Screen Time' Called Health Threat for Kids," *Star Tribune* 1999 Aug. 3: 1A

21. B. Meltz, "Computers, Software can Harm Emotional, Social Development," *Boston Globe*, 1998 Oct. 1, city ed.: F1.

22. L. Helms, "High Tech Sales Reach into Schools," *Los Angeles Times*, 1997 June 9: A-1

23. S. Banks and L. Renwick, "Technology is Still a Promise, Not a Panacea," *Los Angeles Times* 1997 June 8: Orange County Edition, A-1.

24. L. Helm, "High Tech Sales Goals Fuel Reach into Schools," *Los Angeles Times* 1997 June 9: A-1

25. J. Healy, *Failure to Connect* (New York: Touchstone, 1999) 80.

26. J. Healy, "The 'Meme' That Ate Childhood," *Education Week on the Web*, 1998 October 7, http://www.edweek.org/ew/1998/06healy.h18 2003 Mar. 4.

27. Healy, *Failure to Connect*, 44.

28. J. Archer, "The Link to Higher Scores," *Education Week's 'Technology Counts'"* 1998 Sept. http://www.edweek.org/sreports/tc98/ets/ets-n.htm 2003 March 21.

29. T. Oppenheimer, "The Computer Delusion," *The Atlantic Monthly* 280.1 (1997 July): 45-62.

30. "Computers Won't Fix Schools," (editorial) *Los Angeles Times*, 1997 Dec. 28.

31. "Computer's Role in Education," *Learning in the Real World*, (n.d.). http://www.realworld.org/ 2003 Mar. 4.

32. Banks and Renwick.

33. D. Ravitch, "The Great Technology Mania," *Forbes* 1998 Mar. 23: 134.

34. Meltz.

35. L. Cuban. "Techno-Reformers and Classroom Teachers," *Education Week on the Web*, 1996 Oct. 9, http://www.edweek.org/ew/vol-16/

06cuban.h16 2003 Mar. 21.

36. "High Tech Heretic: Why Computers Don't Belong in the Classroom and Other Reflections by a Computer Contrarian." (n.d.). http://www.familyhaven.com/parenting/hightechheretic.html 2003 Mar. 4.

37. L. Cuban, "High-Tech Schools and Low-Tech Teaching," *Education Week on the Web*, 1997 May 21. http://www.edweek.org/ew/vol-16/34cuban.h16 2003 Mar. 21.

38. G. Wolf, "Steve Jobs: The Next Insanely Great Thing," *Wired*, 1996 Feb., 104.

39. J. Michaels. Letter. *Forbes* 27Aug. 1984, 4, 156.

Chapter 7

1. "Congressional Briefing: Facts About the Effects of Advertising and Marketing on Children," *Stop Commercial Exploitation of Children,* 2003 Jan. 31, 2003 Apr. 4, http://www.commercialsexploitation.com/articles/congressional_briefing_facts.htm

2. H. Chaplin, "Food Fight," *American Demographic* 21.6 (1999 June): 64-65.

3. L. Chunovic, "Marketers Turning 'Tween' Into Green," *ElectronicMedia* 21.31 (2002 Aug. 5): 6, 22.

4. "GiveAnything.com for Teens," *Link-up* 18.5 (2001 Sept/Oct.): 1, 6.

5. Chaplin.

6. Chunovic.

7. C. Seipp, "KIDS: The New Captive Market," *Judge Baker Children's*, 2001 Sept., 2003 Apr. 19,http://www.jbcc.harvard.edu/media2/press_seipp.htm

8. J. Cooper, "Parents: Kids Know Best," *Mediaweek* 1999 Feb. 8: 14.

9. Seipp.

10. T. McGrath, "Who's Got an Eye on Your Kids?" *U.S. Catholic* 67.1 (2002 Jan.): 50.

11. Seipp.

12. Rutledge.

13. "GiveAnything."

14. K. Rutledge, "Wooing Teens to Buy On Line Has E-tailers Seeing Green," *Discount Store* 39.7 (3 April 2000): 17.

15. M. Irvine, "Poll Finds Strong 'Nag Factor' in Children," *Chicago Tribune*, 18 June 2002: sec. 1, p. 1.

16. Seipp.

17. M. Dolliver, "Parents Need to Tell Kids: You're Not the Boss of Me," *Adweek* 2001 Aug. 13: 28.

18. M. Dolliver, "Sorry, But You Picked the Wrong Century to Raise Kids," *Adweek* 2002 Nov. 4: 30.

19. M. Larson, "Children's Responses to the Images of Children in Television Commercials," National Communication Association Convention, Seattle, 2000 Nov. 9.

20. Irvine.

21. "Merchants of Cool." D. Rushkoff. Frontline. PBS. 2001 Feb. 27.

22. *SoulKool⁻Industrial Strength Promotions* (n.d.), 2003 June 27, <www.soulkool.com

23. "The Power of Peer Pressure," *Newsweek* 2002 Dec. 23: 9.

24. K. Bedford, "Pediatricians Again Advise Against TV for Very Young Kids," *Current Online* 1999 Aug. 28, 2002 Oct. 20, http:// www.current.org/ch/ch915p.html

25. D. Buss, "Making Your Mark in Movies and TV," *Nation's Business* 1998 Dec.: 28-32.

26. D. Darlin, "Junior Mints, I'm Gonna Make You a Star," *Forbes* 1995 Nov. 6: 90-94.

27. G. Cebrzynski, "Panda Express Lands Roles in Movies, Hit TV Show," *Nation's Restaurant News* 2002 Feb. 11: 6.

28. N. Labi, "Classrooms for Sale," *Time* 153.15 (1999 Apr. 19): 44-45.

29. S. Bell, "Commercialism in Schools: An Interview with the Center for Commercial-Free Public Education," *Radical Teacher* 55 (1999): 4-8.

30. A. Molnar, "Fifth Annual Report on Commercialism in Schools/The Corporate Branding of Our Schools," *Educational Leadership* 60.2 (2002): 74-79.

31. A. Molnar and J. Reaves, "Buy Me! Buy Me!" *Educational Leadership* 59.2 (2001): 74-80.

32. S. Manning, "The Littlest Coke Addicts," *The Nation* 272.5 (2001 June 25): 7-8.

33. S. Manning, "Students for Sale," *The Nation* 269.9 (1999 Sept. 27): 11-13.

34. P. King, "Corporate Sponsorships can Serve a Valuable Purpose," *Nation's Restaurant News* 31.15 (1997 Apr. 14): 16.

35. Manning, "Students."

36. A. Stark, "Pizza Hut, Domino's, and the Public Schools," *Policy Review* 108 (2001 Aug./Sept.): 59-71.

37. Seipp.

38. Manning, "Students."

39. Molnar and Reeves.

40. Molnar.

41. "In-Your-Face Advertising," *The Commercial Appeal*, 2003 Feb. 19: sec. B, p. 4.

42. Molnar.

43. Stark.

44. "Debt Nation," *News Hour Extra*, 2001 Apr., 2003 Apr. 28, http://www.pbs.org/newshour/extra/features/jan-june01/credit_debt.html

45. "Why Don't Parents Talk?" *The Mint* 2002, 2003 Apr. 28, http://www.themint.org/parents/talktoyourkids.php

46. "Debt Nation."

47. "About College Student Debt," *The Mint* 2002, 2003 Apr. 28, http://www.themint.org/owing/students.php

48. "Annual U.S. Non-Business Bankruptcy Filings by Chapter and Judicial District 2000-2001," *ABI World*, 2003 Apr. 28, http://www.abiworld.org/stats/2000annualnonbuschapter.html

49. "The Parent's Role," *The Mint* 2002, 2003 Apr. 28, http://www.themint.org/parents/index.php

Chapter 8

1. M. Dickerson, "Parents, Take Charge of Kids' Video Games," *Seattle Post-Intelligencer*, 2002 Dec. 20: B9.

2. "Understanding the Rating System," *Media Awareness Network* 2003, 2003 Apr. 10 http://www.media-awareness.ca/english/parents/video_games/ratings_videogames.cfm

3. "Special Issues for Young Children," *Media Awareness Network* 2003, 2003 May 26, http://www.media-awarenesss.ca/english/parents/video_games/issues_child_videogames.cfm

4. D. Walter, "Video Game Ordinance Considered Unconstitutional," *St. Louis Daily Record/St. Louis Countian*, 2003 June 5: NEWS.

5. "Violence," *Media Awareness Network* 2003, 2003 April 10, http://www.media-awareness.ca/english/parents/video_games/concerns/violence_videogames.cfm

6. B. Weaver, "Violent Games Pushing Buttons: An Inland Lawmaker Joins Critics Seeking to Prevent Some Titles from Reaching Kids," *The Press Enterprise*, 2003 Jan. 20: B01.

7. E. O'Keefe, "Violent Video Games Still Reach Kids," *abcNEWS.com* 2001 Dec. 13, 2003 Apr. 4, http://abcnews.go.com/sections/scitech/DailyNews/videogames011213.html

8. P. Peck, "Violent Video Games Shown to Affect Brain Cells, *UPI Science News,* 2002 Dec. 2, 2003 Feb. 25, http://www.rense.com/general32/brainc.htm

9. S. Barr, "Computer Violence: Are Your Kids at Risk?" *Reader's Digest* 2001, 2003 Mar. 28, *http://www.rd.com/print_page.jtml?articleId=9519993*

10. S. Greenspan, "Media Effects on Children: Video Games," *Preteenagers Today* 1999-2002, 2002 Sept. 9, http://preteenagers.com/resources/articles/videogames.htm

11. J. Fussell, "Mind-warping Game Violence: Exactly, Say Critics," *The Record,* 2003 Mar. 11: F01.

12. M. Rich, "Violent Video Games Testimony," Chicago City Council, 30, 2000 Oct.

13. Peck.

14. Fussell.

15. D. Grossman, "SKIRMISHER Interview," *SKIRMISHER Online Gaming* magazine (n.d.), 2003 Jan. 12, http://www.skirmisher.com/grossint.htm

16. Barr.

17. D. Phau, "Studies Show Violent Videos Damage Brain," *The Schiller Institute,* 2002 Dec. 27, 2003 Mar. 12, http://www.schiller institute.org/new_viol/videos_brain.html.

18. D. Grossman, *Stop Teaching Our Kids to Kill* (New York: Crown, 1999) 4, 75-76.

19. "Group Cites Video Games for Violence Against Women," *Record Searchlight,* 2002 Dec. 20, 2003 June 13, http://www.redding.com/news/national/past/20021220nat025.shtml

20. "Gender Stereotyping," *Media Awareness Network* 2003, 2003 Apr. 10, http://www.media-awareness.ca/english/parents/video_games/concerns/violence_videogames.cfm

21. C. Anderson and K. Dill, "Video Games and Aggressive Thoughts, Feelings and Behavior in the Laboratory and in Life," *Journal of Personality and Social Psychology* 78.4(April 2000): 772-790.

22. P. Sabga, "A New Study Questions the Medical Effects of Video Games," *Today* , NBC, 2002 Dec. 19.

23. Rich.

24. Sabga.

25. Weaver.

26. Barr.

27. Greenspan.

28. D. Grossman, *Stop* 72-73.

29. *Fair Play? Violence, Gender and Race in Video Games,* (Oakland CA: 2001).

30. Children Now.

31. "Gender Stereotyping."

32. C. Morris, "Bikes, Sex and Volleyball," cnnmoney, 2002 Sept. 17, 2003 May 26, http://money.cnn.com/2002/09/16/commentary/game_over/column_gaming

33. B. Berkowitz, "Report Condemns Sex, Violence in Video Games," *Impact Wrestling* 2002 Dec. 20, 2003 June 13, http://www.impactwrestlingonline.com/game.asp?vidcon=51

34. Children Now.

35. Children Now.

36. D. Brown, "Change the Game," *The Source* Dec. 2001, 2003 June 17, http://www.geocities.com/nomadgames/dec01source.html

37. D. Brown.

38. M. Marriott, "Blood, Gore, Sex and Now: Race," *Technology/Circuits,* 1999 Oct. 21, 2003 June 17, http://www.nytimes.com/library/tech/99/10/circuits/articles/21skin.html

39. D. Brown.

40. Marriott, "Blood."

41. Children Now.

42. Marriott, "Blood."

43. Children Now.

44. Children Now.

45. Marriott, "Blood."

46. M. Marriott, "Game Formula Is Adding Sex to the Mix," *The New York Times*, 2002 Nov. 7: G1.

47. J. Stossel, "The Games Kids Play," *abcNEWS.com,* 2000 Mar. 22, 2003 Mar. 28, http://abcnews.go.com/onair/2020/2020_000322_videogames_feature.html

48. K. Rutledge, "Wooing Teens to Buy On Line Has E-tailers Seeing Green," *Discount Store* 39.7 (2000 Apr. 3): 17.

49. J. Lawrence, "Lethal Recreations: How Violent Computer Games Can Affect the Teenage Brain," *The Independent*, 2003 Jan. 8: NEWS 13.

50. Anderson and Dill.

51. J. Brown, "Doom, Quake and Mass Murder," *Salon Technology* 1999 Apr. 23, 2003 Mar. 28, http://www.salon.com/tech/feature/1999/04/23/gamers.html

Chapter 9

1. "Tracking Cyber-Predators," *CBSNEWS.com,* 2000 Mar. 22, 2003 Nov. 16, http://www.cbsnews.com/stories/2000/03/22/48hours/main174929.shtml

2. "Remarks by Vice President Al Gore at the Internet/Online Summit," 1997 Dec. 2, 2003 Nov. 21, http://www.usdoj.gov/crimial/cybercrime/gore-sp.htm

3. R. Nordland and J. Bartholet, "The Web's Dark Secret," *Newsweek,* 2001 Mar. 19: 44-51.

4. R. O'Grady, "Eradicating Pedophilia: Toward the Humanization of Society," *Journal of International Affairs* 55.1 (2001 Fall): 123-140.

5. "Risks for Parents to Be Aware," n.d., 2003 Nov. 20, http://userpages.umbc.edu/~chris2/403cs/Risks.htm

6. "Protecting Kids Online," *Washingtonpost.com Online Chat,* 2001 Sept. 6, 2003 Nov. 29, http://www.protectkids.com/donnaricehughes interview_washingtonpost090601.htm

7. L. Dewey, "Girls Online: Feeling Out of Bounds," *Camping* magazine 75.5 (2002 Sept./Oct.): 48-50.

8. S. Kelly, "Chat Room Dangers," *BBC World,* 2003 Sept. 4, 2003 Nov. 16, http://www.bbcworld.com/content clickonline_archive_35_2003.asp?pageid=666&co_pageid=3

9. "The Effects of Pornography and Sexual Messages," *National Coalition for the Protection of Children & Families* n.d., 2002 Sept. 29, http://www.nationalcoalition.org/pornhamr.phtml?ID=102

10. "Microsoft Chat Move 'Irresponsible,'" *BBC News,* 2003 Sept. 24, 2003 Nov. 16, http://news.bbc.co.uk/go/pr/fr/-/2/hi/technology/3136006.stm

11. N. Bernstein, "THE LIST—A special report: On Prison Computer, Files to Make Parents Shiver," *The New York Times,* 1996 Nov. 18, A1.

12. J. Cusack, "The Murky World of Internet Porn.," *World Press Review* 43 (Nov. 1996): 8-9.

13. Nordland and Bartholet.

14. K. Durkin, "Misuse of the Internet by Pedophiles: Implications for Law Enforcement and Probation Practice," *Federal Probation* 61 (1997 Sept.): 14-18.

15. "Tracking."

16. H. Stringer, "CyberXXX," *Techweek,* 2000 Sept. 19, 2003 Nov. 30, http://www.techweek.com

17. J. Burris, "No Single Solution for Protecting Kids from Internet Pornography," *The National Academies,* 2002 May 2, 2003 Nov. 30, http

18. "How Pornography Harms Children," *ProtectKids.com* 2001, 2003 Apr. 2, http://www.protectkids.com/effects/harms.htm

19. Kelly.

20. Kelly.

21. T. Strode, "Internet Pornography Use Common in Many Libraries, Report Says," *ChristianityToday.com* 2000, 2003 Nov. 28, http://www.christianitytoday.com/ct/2000/112/23.0.html

22. Kelly.

23. "Extent of the Problem," n.d., 2003 Nov. 28, http://www.familyschoice.com/main/extent-stats.htm

24. L. Clark, "ALA Denounces Supreme Court Ruling on Children's Internet Protection Act," *American Library Assocation*, 2003 June 23, 2003 Nov. 28, http://www.ala.org/Template.cfm?Section=News&template=/ContentManagement/ContentDisplay.cfmContentID=36161

25. E. Ramirez, "Berkeley Library to Reject Web Filter Software," *TheDaily Californian*, 2001 Oct. 31, 2003 Nov. 28, http://www.dailycal.org/article.asp?id=6895

26. T. Loci, "Lost Innocence," *U.S. News & World Report* 129.8 (2000 Aug. 28): 38-39.

27. A. Van Buren, "Predators Stalking the Internet," *Chicago Tribune*, 2003 Oct. 29: Tempo, Sec. 5, p. 9.

28. A. Van Buren, "Child Lured to Obsessive Relationship," *TwinCities.com* 2003 Oct. 30, 2003 Nov. 21, http://www.philly.com/mld/twincities/living/7132617.htm

29. A. Lenhart, L. Rainie, and O. Lewis, *Teenage Life Online: The Rise of the Instant-Message Generation and the Internet's Impact on Friendships and Family Relationships*, (Washington D.C.: Pew Internet & American Life Project, 2001).

30. Lenhart, Rainie and Lewis.

31. P. Festa, "Teen Accused of IM Harassment," *c/net NEWS.COM*, 2002 May 15, 2003 Jan. 14, http://news.com.com/2102-1023-914471.html

32. R. Simmons, "Cliques, Clicks, Bullies and Blogs," *Washington Post*, 2003 Sept. 28, B01.

33. "Conversations with Teens About Tech, Part 1: Instant-Messaging," *Net Family News,* 2002 May 15, 2003 Jan. 14, http://www.netfamilynews.org/n1030425.html

34. D. McGuire, "Spammers Target Instant Message Users" *Washingtonpost.com* 2003, 2004 Jan. 31 2004, http://www.computersops.biz/article4094.html

35. J. Leishman, "Cyber-bullying: The Internet is the Latest Weapon in a Bully's Arsenal," *CBCnews: The National,* 2002 Oct. 10, 2003 Nov. 20, http://www.cbc.ca/national/news/cyberbullying/cyber_bullying.html

36. Durkin.

37. "Child Pornography Exists on the Internet," Child Protection Society n.d., 2004 Feb. 3, http://www.geocities.com/CapitolHill/5021/

38. E. Meera, "McGill Study to Examine Internet Gambling," *themuse.ca* 2003 Nov. 27, 2003 Dec. 2, http://www.themuse.ca/national/index.php?articleid=1404&printable=1

39. "Teens Gambling Through Internet," *CBC.CA News,* 2003 Mar. 14, 2003 Nov. 20, http://www.cbc.ca/cgi-bin/templates/print.cgi?/2003/02/27Consumers/teengamblers_030227

40. "Internet Gambling is No Game for Teens,"*Performance Resource Press, Inc.* 2001, 2003 Nov. 16, http://www.prponline/net/Work/HS/Articles/internet_gambling_is_no_game_for_teens.htm

41. "Teens Gambling Through Internet," *CBC.CA,* 2003 Mar. 14, 2003 Nov. 20, http://www.cbc.ca/cgi-bin/templates/print.cgi?/2003.02/27/Consumers/teengamblers_030227

42. "Don't Bet on It: Internet Gambling a Growing Threat," *Congressman Spencer Bachus,* 2002, 1 Oct.1, 2003 Dec. 2, http://bachus.house.gov/NR/23654940-92AC-4F4B-8DDE-B87766AAFE16.htm

43. D. Levin and S. Arafeh, *The Digital Disconnect: The Widening Gap Between Internet-Savvy Students and Their Schools* (Washington D.C.: Pew Internet & American Life Project, 2002 Aug. 14)

44. Levin and Arafeh.

45. P. Mendels, "Hate Groups Target Children and Women Online," *HURINet,* 1999 June 28, 2003 Nov. 20, http://www.hrea.org/lists/huridocs-tech/markup/msg00181.html

46. "Hate Groups Target Children and Women Online," *The Human Rights Information Network,* 1999 June 28, 20003 Nov. 20, http://www.human-rights.net/huridocs-tech.

47. "Stormfront," 2001, 2004 Feb. 6 http://www.reed.edu/~gronkep/webofpolitics/fall2001/yagern/stormfront.html

48. N. Hunt, "Hate Groups Seek to Recruit Through Internet," *Reuters,* 1999 July 5, 2003 Nov. 15, http://www.rickross.com/reference/hate_groups/hategroups79.html

49. "Hate Groups."

50. M. Jenkin, "Be Aware of Hate Groups," *Eastern Poconos Community News,* 2003 Oct. 24, 2003 Nov. 15, http://www.epcommunitynews.com/archives/2003/mj102403.htm

Chapter 10

1. E. Black, "TV 101: Teaching Kids How to Watch Wisely," *Minneapolis Star Tribune*, 1997 Oct. 6, A1, A10.

2. "Food for Thought: Making Food Look Good," *Media Awareness Network* 2003, 2003 Dec. 18, http://www.media-awareness.ca/english/resources/educational/handouts/advertising_marketing/food_ads.cfm

3. G. Goodale, "Execs Say Some Ideas Are Too Much for Reality TV," *The News Tribune—Tacoma WA,* 2003 Jan., 2003 Dec. 20, http://www.tribnet.com/24hour/entertainment/story/738899p-5376436.html

4. Black.

5. A. Franken, *Lies (and the Lying Liars Who Tell Them* (New York: Dutton, 2003) 58-64.

6. "Who Owns What?" *Columbia Journalism Review,* 2003 Oct. 8, 2003 Dec. 21, http://www.cjr.org/tools/owners/

7. NOW Foundation, "Watch Out Listen Up!" 2002 Feminist Prime Time Report. Retrieved July 2, 2008 from http://www.nowfoundation.org/issues/communications/watchout3/report.pdf

Index

About the Author

Mary Strom Larson has been a professor of Communications at Northern Illinois University since 1985. She has regularly taught courses in "Media and Society" and "The Media, Children and Adolescents." She has presented 26 papers

Mary Strom Larson

Photo courtesy of Lou Herout

at professional meetings and published 18 articles in scholarly journals on these topics. Her most requested articles have been "Sex Roles and Soap Operas: What Adolescents Learn About Single Motherhood," "Family Communication on Prime Time Television" (a comparison of the Simpsons and the Huxtables) and "Interactions Between Siblings in Primetime Television Families." Her most recent publications are "Race and Interracial Relationships in Children's

continued

Television Commercials," and "Gender, Race and Agression in Television Commercials" and "Gender, Race and Aggression in Television Commercials that Feature Children." She has been featured on National Public Radio's *Todd Mundi Show*, WIFR television, *Christian Science Monitor*, *Washington Post*, *First for Women*, *Chicago Parent*, *Chicago Southtown Economist*, and numerous local and regional publications. She appeared at the Chicago Cultural Center with TV Moms June Cleaver, Shirley Partridge and Joan Nash in a panel titled, "From My Little Margie to Murphy Brown: Images of Women on Television." She has also presented "Television and the Adolescent Issues of Particular Importance to the Medical Community" to Pediatric Interns at the University of Illinois College of Medicine. She has served on the Media Literacy Task Force of the NCA.

Says practical educator in Mary, "When my older daughter was about eight or so, her bickering sounded just like Lucy in the Charlie Brown books, and I forbade her to read them. She and her sister claimed this was totally stupid. But I did it anyway!"

Mary has lived in an historic home in Sycamore, Illinois, for thirty-plus years, and she and her husband have devoted their spare time and energy restoring and maintaining the beautiful, old house with its large gardens.